MYSTIC SEAFOOD

MYSTIC SEAFOOD

GREAT RECIPES, HISTORY, AND SEAFARING LORE FROM MYSTIC SEAPORT

JEAN KERR with **SPENCER SMITH**

ThreeForks™

GUILFORD, CONNECTICUT
HELENA, MONTANA

AN IMPRINT OF THE GLOBE PEQUOT PRESS

ThreeForks is a trademark of Morris Book Publishing, LLC.

Photo credits: See pp. 199–200.
Text design by Nancy Freeborn

Library of Congress Cataloging-in-Publication Data

Kerr, Jean, 1958-
  Mystic seafood : great recipes, history, and seafaring lore from Mystic Seaport /
Jean Kerr with Spencer Smith.
     p. cm.
  Includes index.
  ISBN-13: 978-0-7627-4137-3
  ISBN-10: 0-7627-4137-6
  1. Cookery (Seafood)   2. Mystic Seaport, Inc.   I. Smith, Spencer, 1948-   II. Title.
  TX747.K457 2006
  641.6'92—dc22
                                    2006029646

Manufactured in the United States of America
First Edition/First Printing

FOR MY DAD,

WHO NEVER MET AN OYSTER HE DIDN'T LIKE.

Catboat *Breck Marshall* nestles just off the bow of the *Joseph Conrad* at Mystic Seaport.

Contents

Acknowledgments

We are indebted to so many people for their help and support including:

The knowledgeable and enthusiastic staff of Mystic Seaport including Amy German, Kelly Drake, Mary Anne Stets, Steve Souza, and Louisa Watrous.

Karen Billipp who was helpful in so many ways.

Laura Strom and Elizabeth Taylor of Globe Pequot Press for their dedication to the project. Ace copyeditor Laura Jorstad whose attention to detail and unflagging cheer helped so much in creating this book. Kara Steere, eagle-eyed proofreader and Kathleen Rocheleau, indexer.

We would also like to thank the many people who provided information and inspiration including Linda Greenlaw, Kathy Gunst, Mary Ann Esposito, James Haller, Steve White, Joe Milano and Mary Ann Milano Picardi of the Union Oyster House, Dave Kaselauskas, and Sandy Oliver. Thanks to Jean Somers for providing great resources.

Our thanks go to our recipe testers Paula Sullivan, Eva Baughman, Diane Giese, my dear friend Parkie Boley, and David, Moe, and Casey Halle. A special thanks to Kyle Herwig who's going to be a star chef one day. Thanks to all our friends who tasted seafood after seafood meal with patient good humor.

We are grateful to all the great chefs who kindly shared their wonderful dishes with us. We urge you to visit their establishments and taste their creations first hand. Many thanks to those who provided us with the wonderful raw materials for these recipes: Browne Trading Company, Sunny's Seafood, York Lobster and Seafood, Sue's Seafood, Olde Mill Fish Market, Ducktrap River Fish Farm, and the Municipal Fish Market, Lagos, Portugal.

We are also grateful to a number of organizations that so kindly shared their resources with us including The Gloucester Fishermen's Wives Association, the NorthEast Fisheries Science Center, the Maine Lobster Promotion Council, and Maine Lobstermen's Association.

Love and gratitude to my husband Bud Fisher, who ate rather more fish than he would have liked while I worked on these recipes. Thanks also to my mom and the Maryland branch of the Kerrs who provided willing palates and valuable information on blue crabs and oysters. My thanks to Connie and Jerry Held, who provided an opportunity to cook in their incredible kitchen with an endless supply of my favorite chardonnay on hand. Gratitude to the entire Held-Zimmer clan for tasting and appreciating. My thanks also to April Frost, loving and supportive taste tester extraordinaire.

Preface

I have spent most of my life along the New England coast. My earliest summers were full of small adventures in rowboats and skiffs, which later became a bit bigger as I progressed to larger boats and sailing the Maine coast. We dug clams, picked mussels, and caught flounder and striped bass. Family and friends would gather for big lobster dinners in the summertime, the kids sucking the meat out of the legs, until we warranted our own whole lobster instead of hot dogs. In late summer we walked just up the road for fresh-picked corn to accompany our feasts.

We knew the fishermen and how our food was caught. We debated the relative merits of lobster claws versus tails and whether it was worth picking out the body meat. My mother, who endured World War II food rationing in Great Britain, was always picking apart the bodies long after everyone else had thrown in the napkin. Anyone fortunate enough to grow up as I did will know that the New England experience—and our history—has everything to do with the ocean and the bounty that comes from it. That's why I fell in love with Mystic Seaport.

When you walk in the gate of Mystic Seaport, you are entering a time capsule of all things related to the sea. Although Mystic Seaport is a rich resource for naval history, its real appeal is in the way it has recreated a typical 1800s coastal village, with fishing boats large and small, along with a faithful facsimile of the day-to-day activities of the time. Not surprisingly, most of these are related to fishing, whaling, and boatbuilding.

Mystic Seaport is home to more than 500 vessels. Standing on the deck of the *Charles W. Morgan*, or sitting at a table in the cabins below, you can cast yourself back to the days of the whaling ships. The *L. A. Dunton*, a Gloucester fishing schooner built in 1921, recalls the days when cod were plentiful. The *Estella A.* is a

Skiff and wooden lobster traps at Mystic Seaport.

Friendship sloop built for a Maine lobsterman before the days of diesel. The *Nellie*, an oyster sloop built in 1891, and the *Regina M.*, a sardine carrier, all help us to understand the many ways in which our seafood came to the shore.

The men and women who fished, tonged, dug, trawled, and trapped fish and shellfish did not have an easy life, but there was something that drew them to the sea, and they left a rich maritime history in their wake. Nowhere is it more dynamically captured than at Mystic Seaport.

This book brings together two of my passions—food and the sea—against the backdrop of our maritime heritage, captured so dramatically at Mystic Seaport. I can't think of two more fundamental influences on my life—the endlessly changing, challenging, spectacular ocean and the comfort, tradition, and inventiveness that cooking allows. I hope these two forces will unite here to bring you both history and an innovative approach to preparing the fruits of the sea.

A NOTE ON THE RECIPES

I've tried to provide a range of recipes, from historic to cutting edge. In my own recipes, my goal has been to keep things simple to let the flavors of the fish shine through. In my conversations with chefs, this is something that kept coming up, though some of their preparations are more complex than anything I could have dreamed up on my own.

One of the biggest challenges in writing this book was creating recipes. Since I generally don't cook using recipes, it was difficult to remember to measure and time things. I hope most of the instructions are clear, but I urge you to experiment according to your own tastes. And by all means, substitute clams for mussels, cod for haddock, swordfish for halibut. Generally, you can substitute any firm fish steak for any other, and any mild white fillets for any other. Have fun with your fish! Get creative!

You'll notice, too, a broad range of ethnic influences on the recipes throughout this book. That should come as no surprise. The New England fisheries have attracted English, Spanish, Portuguese, Italians, and other Europeans since this country was founded. It's natural—and wonderful—that there are so many ethnic influences to keep things interesting. More recently Asian immigrants have come to America to fish, and since fish is such an important part of many Asian cuisines, we now enjoy some wonderful new flavors as well.

In the interest of broadening seafood horizons, some recipes here call for fish that are native to the North Atlantic but are far less common than the usual haddock–cod–swordfish lineup. The more we come to accept and enjoy different types of fish, the more likely we are to have strong, sustainable fisheries. For more information on ocean friendly species, visit www.blueocean.org or search the web for "sustainable fisheries."

PART ONE

ON THE HALF SHELL: BIVALVES

"He had often eaten oysters,
but had never had enough."

—W. S. GILBERT

Oysters

In *The Art of Eating*, M. F. K. Fisher famously remarked: "There are three kinds of oyster eaters: those loose-minded sports who will eat anything, hot, cold, thin, thick, dead or alive, as long as it is an oyster; those who will eat them raw and only raw; and those who with equal severity will eat them cooked and no way other." My father counted himself among the first group—a man who never met an oyster he didn't like.

This was strange to me, as he was born in Lawrence, Massachusetts, in 1916, grew up in the dingy culinary tradition of a Scottish Presbyterian household, and otherwise could hardly be described as "a loose-minded sport." He liked hot dogs, beans, and brown bread; ham sandwiches, roast beef, and mashed potatoes. He had no love of swimming fish, but loved lobsters and shrimp. Watching him eat oysters was something altogether different, though, and a source of wonderful memories. When he ate oysters, a different side of him emerged. He approached oysters with a kind of reverence, savoring the complex briny tastes with great focus. It was a bit like watching someone listen to a favorite symphony. It was the only time I saw my father close his eyes when he ate.

For many years our Christmas dinners would begin with oysters on the half shell, an American tradition that originated in the late 1800s. My brother, the designated shucker, would have brought a peck of bluepoints up from Maryland that morning. After he arrived, presents were opened, then it was on to Bloody Marys and oysters. Then a standing rib roast of beef and plum pudding.

It was a dangerous thing to set the platter of freshly shucked oysters in front of my father—if you wanted any for yourself, that is. Eventually we all wised up and kept some back. Otherwise, by the time my diligent shucker-brother had removed his apron, I had mixed and delivered the Bloody Marys, and my mother had attempted unsuccessfully to fend my father off, the platter would hold perhaps one dozen, out of five or six dozen, for the three of us to share. I remember hearing him call out, "You'd better get in here if you want some of these!"

My father lived a long and happy life. Whether it had anything to do with the oysters, I can't say. I do know that he left us an oyster legacy. Not only do I still love oysters and still savor them as part of our family's traditions, but every time I taste the clear, briny ocean flavor of an oyster on the half shell, I'm offering a sort of tribute to my dad. I close my eyes and taste.

A BRIEF HISTORY OF OYSTERING

Oystering certainly didn't start in the United States—people have been eating oysters since Roman times—but it has been an integral part of the American fishing scene from pre-colonial days.

Native Americans on both coasts ate oysters, as did the colonists, but it was in the nineteenth century that oystering really took off. Oysters were eaten in casseroles, stuffings, and stews. They were popular street food, grilled on braziers and eaten on the run—the nineteenth-century version of a slice of pizza to go. By the late 1800s no elegant dinner was complete without a few dozen bluepoints to start.

To satisfy the American hunger for oysters, oystering became a full-fledged industry. Unlike most fishing, which didn't do much to maintain healthy stock levels, oyster fishermen seeded their own oyster beds, leaving some fallow to prevent overfishing and allow the oysters to grow to marketable size. Oysters grown in polluted waters such as New York Harbor were often moved to cleaner waters in Long Island Sound to purify themselves before they were sent to market. Oystering was almost certainly the first American aquaculture.

"Oysters in Every Style" are available in this nineteenth century restaurant. The bearded gentleman at left is eating them raw as the barman opens them.

Oysters are harvested in shallow water. The traditional method uses tongs, scissorlike metal rakes that grab the oysters and pull them from the bottom. Oystermen stand in a boat's open cockpit and tong the oysters in water about ten feet deep.

Dredging is another technique used for oystering. Dredges were towed along the bottom by sailing vessels such as the Mystic Seaport's *Nellie*. Built in 1891, the *Nellie* was a sailing oyster dredger in southeastern Connecticut and Long Island's Great South Bay. Her flat bottom permitted oystering in shallow waters, while her large sailing rig made her as fast as many yachts and minimized the time spent getting back and forth to the oyster beds.

KNOW YOUR OYSTERS

Although there are dozens of kinds of oysters in the United States, there are only four actual varieties. These four are, however, spread over such a wide range of coastline that they develop distinct local tastes and textures.

The eastern oyster is known by many names: the Bluepoint (New York), Malpeque (Prince Edward Island), Chincoteague (Virginia), Breton Sound (Louisiana), Wellfleet (Massachusetts), and Cotuit (Massachusetts), among others. Eastern oysters are eaten both cooked and raw. Those hailing from the colder waters in Canada and New England are usually firmer and somewhat brinier in taste. They are eaten year-round, although some folks feel that they are softer and less tangy in the summer months—the "non-R" months.

The Belon or European oyster is raised both in the United States and throughout Europe. It is native to Brittany and eaten raw, not cooked. To many it is the finest oyster for eating on the half shell. Belons, like Pacifics and Olympias, spawn during the summer months, which causes their taste and texture to be less appealing.

Nellie at Mystic Seaport. Her wide decks and shallow hull made her a good working platform for oystering in the shallow waters of Long Island Sound.

The Olympia oyster is native to Washington's Puget Sound but is found from Alaska to Mexico. It is small with a full, coppery taste and is eaten raw, not cooked.

The Pacific or Japanese oyster is the giant of the oyster family, sometimes reaching a foot in length. Although the larger specimens are too large for eating raw, the smaller ones are very good on the half shell. The flavor is sweet and mild. Because Pacifics grow so rapidly, they are cultivated throughout the world: on the West Coast of the United States as well as in Japan, Chile, and New Zealand.

Oddly, the tiny and delicate Kumamoto oyster is part of the Pacific family of much larger oysters. It is prized for its mild and creamy flavor on the half shell. Because it doesn't spawn in cold American waters, it is eaten year-round.

[right] Tonging for oysters. Like a giant pair of scissors with a rake at the bottom, the tongs pull oysters from the beds.

[below] Mystic Seaport's sharpie skiff *W.B.*, a smaller version of the boats designed to tong for oysters in very shallow waters.

OYSTERS ON THE HALF SHELL

If you've never done it before, opening a raw oyster can be a real challenge. Frankly, it can be challenging even if you have. Not only is it difficult to see where you might insert a tool to pry the shell open, but the seal between the two shells is also very tight. Keep at it, and it'll get easier. It's a skill worth having.

You'll need an oyster knife, which has a long, flat blade with a rounded tip and a large handle.

The basic method is this: Find a sturdy glove or towel in which to hold the oyster. Place the oyster firmly on a flat surface with the flatter shell up and the hinged, narrow end toward you. Pushing firmly, wiggle an oyster knife into the hinge until the knife pushes past the hinge. Give the knife a quarter turn to break the seal. Run the knife against the top shell to disconnect it and discard the top shell. Then run the knife under the oyster to disconnect it from the bottom shell so it will slide out easily—onto a fork or directly into your mouth. The liquid in the shell should be clear and briny, and the oyster should smell like the ocean.

Here are a couple of alternate techniques that, though frowned on by oyster pros, work fairly well:

1. Use an old-fashioned V-shaped, hand-punch can opener to pry the oyster open at the hinge.

2. Hang the wide end over the end of the counter and chip off a piece of the shell with a hammer. Insert an oyster knife into the chip, and pry open by twisting the knife.

Serve oysters on a bed of shaved ice with lemon wedges and your favorite sauce.* This is the method most common to New England. When you get near the Chesapeake, shuckers tend to open from the other end or the side—an even more challenging technique. You can also ask your fishmonger to shuck some oysters for you, but they should be eaten as soon as possible. An oyster on the half shell should be fresh, fresh, fresh.

See sauce recipes on the following page.

MIGNONETTE SAUCE

This is a classic French sauce that seems to be preferred by oyster purists. It really does let the oyster flavor shine. Essentially, you are pickling minced shallots here, so make the sauce at least a couple of hours before you serve it. Invest in a good-quality vinegar—this will be smoother than a less expensive one.

2 tablespoons peppercorns—
    black or a mixture of pink,
    white, and black
2 shallots, minced
2/3 cup red wine vinegar or sherry
    vinegar

1. Crush or grind the peppercorns and place them in a small jar.
2. Add the shallots and vinegar to the jar and shake well.
3. Chill for 2 hours or more.
4. Spoon onto raw oysters, to taste.

MAKES ABOUT 3/4 CUP

COCKTAIL SAUCE

You can experiment with this recipe by using fresh herbs (I like dill and chives) and different kinds of hot sauces. One of my favorites is Tabasco brand Chipotle Pepper Sauce, which is milder and smokier than the company's regular hot sauce.

1/2 cup ketchup
1/3 cup prepared horseradish
2 tablespoons fresh-squeezed
    lemon juice
Fresh-ground pepper, sea salt,
    and hot sauce, to taste

Mix all the ingredients in a small bowl and serve alongside raw oysters or any cold shellfish.

MAKES ABOUT 1 CUP

BLOODY MARY

Oysters on the half shell seem to go beautifully with crisp white wines, such as Muscadets and dry Rieslings, but I love Bloody Marys with mine. Here's my recipe for this classic cocktail that pairs well with just about any kind of seafood appetizer.

4 ounces tomato juice

4 ounces Clamato® juice

2 teaspoons Worcestershire sauce

1 teaspoon prepared horseradish

1 teaspoon fresh lemon juice

Dash of hot sauce

2 ounces vodka

Salt and pepper

Mix all the ingredients and pour into a tall glass over ice. Garnish with a wedge of lime, and a celery stalk or olives.

SERVES 1

Note: You can multiply this recipe by the number of guests and make a pitcher to save time.

This lovely decorated oyster shell comes from a trade card advertising Sans Aretes Cod and its local agent Caswell, Livermore & Co.

"CALIFORNIA ROLL" OYSTERS

This topping—an interesting departure from the usual oyster sauces—evokes the flavors of sushi-bar California rolls, with avocado, wasabi, and fish roe.

½ avocado

2 teaspoons fresh lemon juice

2 teaspoons prepared wasabi

Sea salt, to taste

1 dozen oysters on the half shell

Salmon roe or red lumpfish

1. Mash the avocado well in a bowl.
2. Add the lemon juice and wasabi and mix well. Salt to taste.
3. Top oysters on the half shell with this mixture—about ½ teaspoon each.
4. Sprinkle with fish roe.

MAKES ENOUGH TO TOP A DOZEN OYSTERS ON THE HALF SHELL

FANCY ROAST OYSTERS

This is an adapted version of one of dozens of recipes for oysters from the 1896 *Boston Cooking School Cookbook*. By the time this cookbook was published, oysters were far more popular and presentable on the table than they had been a century and a half earlier, in colonial times. Like lobsters, as oysters became scarcer, they became more prized. In the 1787 *Compleat American Housewife,* oysters are mentioned only once; the Boston Cooking School Cookbook included nearly three dozen preparations.

3 tablespoons butter

1 pint shucked oysters, drained

Sliced brown bread

⅓ cup chopped parsley

Salt and pepper, to taste

1. Melt the butter in a saucepan or frying pan.
2. Add the oysters and sauté them in the butter until they plump up and their edges begin to curl. Shake the pan gently to be sure the oysters cook evenly.
3. Serve the oysters on toasted brown bread cut into triangles and sprinkle with parsley. Season to taste with salt and pepper.

SERVES 6 AS A FIRST COURSE

ANGELS ON HORSEBACK

This is a recipe that has been around for ages, and most versions call for wrapping a shucked oyster in bacon and grilling it. I like the idea of broiling the oysters in their shells on top of the bacon and adding a pinch of Old Bay Seasoning.

12 oysters in the shell

3 slices thick-cut smoky bacon

Pinch of Old Bay Seasoning

Lemon slices, for serving

1. Preheat the oven broiler.

2. Scrub the oyster shells thoroughly under cold running water with a wire brush.

3. Shuck the oysters, reserving each bottom shell. Place these shells in a baking pan on a bed of rock salt or crumpled foil to keep them flat.

4. Chop the bacon slices into 2-inch lengths or to fit a shell lengthwise. Place one piece in each shell.

5. Broil until the bacon curls and renders its fat.

6. Place one oyster in each shell and turn to coat it with bacon fat. Broil until the oysters are just cooked through and curled at the edges, about a minute.

7. Remove the pan from the broiler and add a sprinkle of Old Bay Seasoning on each oyster. Serve with lemon slices.

SERVES 4 AS AN APPETIZER

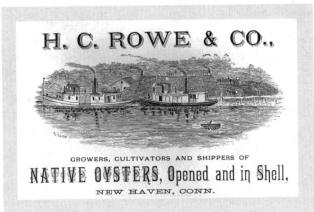

GREAT AMERICAN OYSTER HOUSES

The Union Oyster House

The Union Oyster House at 41 Union Street in Boston is the oldest oyster bar in America—and the nation's oldest restaurant in continuous service as well. Its doors have been open since 1826, when the semicircular oyster bar was installed. It was here that Daniel Webster, a regular customer, drank a tall tumbler of brandy and water with his oysters, generally consuming at least six plates' worth. John F. Kennedy was a patron as well.

You can still get a stool at the bar and watch the expert shuckers opening oysters and clams, and serving up their classic chowders and oyster stew. The oysters are shucked fresh as you watch, and you concoct your own cocktail sauce from jars of ketchup, horseradish, and hot sauce. The oyster bar is a classic, and the model for many other venerable establishments across the country.

In 2003 the Union Oyster House was designated a National Historic Landmark.

Other Great Oyster Houses

Oyster houses don't rely on atmosphere to attract customers—the oysters do that—but they all have their own particular ambience. Here is a variety of venerable establishments from coast to coast where you can belly up to the (oyster) bar.

Grand Central Oyster Bar, circa 1913
Lower Level, Grand Central Station
New York, New York

Snockey's Oyster and Crab House, circa 1910
1020 South Second Street
Philadelphia, Pennsylvania

J. W. Faidley, 1886
Lexington Market
203 North Paca
Baltimore, Maryland

Acme Oyster House, 1910
724 Iberville Street
New Orleans, Louisiana

Shaw's Crab House, 1984
21 East Hubbard
Chicago, Illinois

Swan Oyster Depot, circa 1912
1517 Polk Street
San Francisco, California

Dan & Louis' Oyster Bar, 1907
208 Southwest Ankeny Street
Portland, Oregon

Elliot's Oyster House, circa 1970
1201 Alaskan Way, Pier 56
Seattle, Washington

Boston's Union Oyster House, founded in 1826 and still going strong. The photograph is circa 1880.

OYSTER STEW

Boston's famed Union Oyster House serves this classic oyster stew.

1 pint light cream or half-and-half

2 tablespoons butter

16 raw oysters, freshly shucked,
   with their juices

Paprika or finely chopped parsley

Salt, pepper, Worcestershire
   sauce, and hot sauce, to taste

1. Scald the cream or half-and-half by heating it until a thin skin forms on top.

2. Melt the butter in a small saucepan over low heat.

3. Add the oysters and their juices to the pan and sauté until plumped.

4. Combine the cream, butter, and oysters in a crock or soup bowl.

5. Sprinkle with paprika or parsley. Season to taste with salt, pepper, Worcestershire sauce, and hot sauce.

SERVES 2

Sailing oyster draggers on Chesapeake Bay in 1933.

OYSTERS ROCKEFELLER

Oysters Rockefeller is a classic and luxurious treatment of oysters. Countless chefs have introduced variations on the theme of spinach, bacon, and oysters; this is mine.

2 slices thick-cut bacon

1 tablespoon butter

1 shallot, finely minced

6 cups loosely packed spinach leaves

1 tablespoon Pernod (optional)

1/3 cup whipping cream

12 large oysters on the half shell, drained

2 tablespoons grated Parmesan cheese

1 1/2 tablespoons bread crumbs

Lemon wedges, for serving

1. Preheat the oven broiler.

2. In a large, shallow pan, fry the bacon until just barely crisp. Drain on paper towels and set aside.

3. Pour off all but a couple of teaspoons of the bacon fat. Add the butter to the pan.

4. Sauté the shallot in the fat till it's soft. Add the spinach and cook until just wilted.

5. Add the Pernod, if desired, and cream. Simmer for a minute.

6. Place a spoonful of the topping on each oyster. Top the spinach with a bit of crumbled bacon.

7. Mix the Parmesan and bread crumbs. Sprinkle equally over each oyster.

8. Broil until hot and bubbling. Serve with lemon wedges.

SERVES 4 AS AN APPETIZER

ARE OYSTERS REALLY AN APHRODISIAC?

Oysters as far back as classical Rome were thought to increase vitality, virility, and libido. Legend has it that Casanova used to put away fifty oysters just to start the day and wrote that oysters are "a spur to the spirit and to love." And most oyster aficionados are familiar with the phrase "Eat fish, live longer . . . eat oysters, love longer." While much of the aphrodisiac effect may be just a myth—or a placebo effect—scientists have linked the high zinc content and the presence of two rare amino acids in oysters to increased sexual desire. Whether fact or fiction, the oyster-as-aphrodisiac theory has been around for thousands of years and isn't likely to go away.

"Your remark that clams will lie quiet if music be played to them, was superfluous—entirely superfluous."

—MARK TWAIN

Clams

In April 1884 the *Willimantic Chronicle,* a local Connecticut newspaper reported that Mr. Orwell Atwood was moving for the summer season from his beautiful inland farm in Mansfield Centre to Stonington, near Mystic. The primary reason for the move, the *Chronicle* wrote, was that "the temptation following a favorable tide, to go a clamming . . . would be greater in that locality than at Mansfield Centre."

Many New Englanders can fully understand Mr. Atwood's dedication to clamming. In coastal New England digging clams, eating clams, and having clambakes is summer. And it's been this way since the 1800s. But clams weren't always so popular.

Clams were one of America's original gathered foods. Though huge shell middens attest to the Native American taste for them in just about every coastal region of the country, it would be 200 years or more before clams would be fully appreciated as the tasty morsels they are by the non-native population. Though the first settlers may have recognized clams as a food that might keep hunger at bay, all too often European tastes and perceptions were negatively influenced by what the colonists perceived as "Indian food." Cotton Mather reported that during lean times, "the only food the poor had was acorns, ground-nuts, mussels and clams."

By the late 1800s, though, New Englanders had managed to romanticize the past and had created the popular myth that clambakes were a tradition of peaceable gatherings in which the Natives and settlers shared. There is no evidence that this is true, but clamming and clambakes had become extremely popular outdoor gatherings.

Taking a train to the seaside to a public clambake was a well-documented nineteenth-century pastime. In her wonderful book *Saltwater Foodways,* historian Sandy Oliver says, "Many large clambake pavilions were built after the middle of the century along the southern New England coast, especially near steamer or train terminals or trolley lines." She goes on to note that a "monster clambake" was held in 1864 near the mouth of Quiambaug Cove a little east of Mystic, Connecticut, and was attended by about 1,000 people.

CLAMDIGGER!

When I was a kid, summering in Down East Maine, the local kids would cheerfully try to get a rise out of the summer kids by calling us "Strap hangers!" (subway riders). To which we retorted "Clamdiggers!" Never mind that few of us rode subways and all of us dug clams.

Clams are harvested at low tide, usually on broad tidal beaches called flats. The traditional method is to dig for them using a clam fork—a sort of rake with four flat, foot-long tines, set at a sharp angle to a wooden handle. Veteran clamdiggers usually have their favorite spots, often marked by numerous airholes in the sand. The tines are worked into the sand then the handle pulled back to reveal, one hopes, unbroken clams that can be pulled out of the sandy pile. These are placed in a clam hod—a wooden frame with a mesh or slatted basket allowing the clams to be easily rinsed in seawater.

Clam digging can be hard on the back, but it's a New England tradition.

Even after several rinses in the hod, however, it's a good idea to let the clams sit for a few hours in seawater (or a gallon of water with $\frac{1}{2}$ cup of sea salt dissolved in it). Some people add a cup of cornmeal to the water to help the clams rid themselves of sand and grit.

Clams are susceptible to "red tide"—a toxin that affects mussels, too. See the warning below.

WHAT'S RED TIDE—AND SHOULD I BE WORRIED?

The ocean is full of algae—microscopic plants that live and die unnoticed by humans. Given the right mixture of sun, temperature, and nutrients, however, algae can "bloom," rapidly multiplying. Most algae remain inoffensive, even when they bloom, but the *Alexandrium tamarense,* a one-celled phytoplankton, is the cause of red tide—and it's a real troublemaker.

Red tide doesn't bother fish, lobsters, or shrimp, but it does accumulate in filter feeders such as oysters, clams, and mussels. When eaten by humans these contaminated bivalves can cause paralytic shellfish poisoning (PSP), resulting in severe illness and even death, although no deaths from red tide have been recorded in New England.

The effects of PSP come on quite rapidly after eating tainted shellfish and may resemble drunkenness. Get the infected person to a hospital without delay.

Fortunately, the coastal waters of the United States are constantly monitored for red tide by a network of government agencies and dedicated volunteers. When a red tide bloom is detected, shellfish beds are posted and closed, and sales are prohibited.

So if you're eating bivalves in a restaurant or buying them from a fishmonger, don't think twice about red tide. If you are collecting your own clams, oysters, or mussels, look for posted warnings and check your state government's web site for red tide information.

SIZE MATTERS

Although there are dozens of varieties of clams in the United States, East Coast clams fall into two major categories: hard shell and soft shell. Hard-shell clams come under the heading of quahog (pronounced *KO-hog*), which is a derivation of its Algonquian name. Clams in this category are classified by size. Littlenecks, named for Littleneck Bay in Long Island, are the smallest and considered by many to be the tastiest to eat raw on the half shell. Cherrystones, after Cherrystone Creek in Virginia, are midsize, and quahogs the largest. These are primarily used for sauces, chowders, and stuffings.

Soft-shell or steamer clams are generally used for frying or eating steamed with butter. In addition to New England soft-shell clams, razor clams—named for their resemblance to an old-time straight razor—are also excellent steamed but are not nearly as common as plain old steamers.

CLAMBAKES—A NEW ENGLAND TRADITION

We do our clambakes at the beach. A beach isn't a requirement, of course; a back yard is fine, but it will be a different experience. I think it's nice to have seawater available for cooking, washing, and swimming. If you're lucky enough to live near a public beach, or have shoreline access, you can usually pull off a fine clambake with a little planning and a permit from the local fire department. Don't neglect the fire regulations—nothing ruins a good clambake like having the authorities show up when everything is half cooked and insist you douse the fire.

I always thought our clambakes were pretty unorthodox in that we steamed everything in a large metal trash can. (I am quick to point out to new guests that this is "the clambake can" and is not used for any other purpose.) It turns out that while the trash can thing is unusual, "cooking in the washtub" is pretty common—at least in Down East Maine—and a good deal simpler (and less sandy) than the traditional method of digging a pit, lining it with stones, building a large wood fire, burning the wood down to heat the stones, adding seaweed and food, covering it all with a wet

A clambake at Mystic, Connecticut, around 1900. Staples such as oysters and corn on the cob can be seen on the table at right.

tarpaulin and steaming it for hours. That takes the best part of a day—my way takes only the best part of an afternoon. Should you wish to take the purist's route, however, there are excellent instructions in *The Joy of Cooking.*

Here's my method. We start out by scrubbing, but not peeling, Yukon Gold potatoes and wrapping each in foil. Allow one medium potato per person. Then we shuck the corn by pulling off the darker green leaves of the husk, and pulling back but not detaching the softer inner leaves to reveal the corn silk. Pull the silk off and wrap the inner husk back around each ear. This protects the sweet kernels and makes a convenient handle when pulled back after cooking. Corn shucking is a good task to delegate; with a cold beverage in hand, most people are happy to help.

Around this time we dig the fire pit. It's about one foot deep and three feet across. Lining the pit with big flat rock keeps the moisture out and gives the pot something firm to sit on. Build a good hot wood fire in the pit, preferably using enough hardwood to keep the fire going for a couple of hours. It's got to be hot enough to boil seawater, which—because of its salt content—boils at a higher temperature than unsalted water.

Next, fill a big tub with ice, beer, maybe a few bottles of white wine, and anything else people might want to drink. Then head off to collect a bushel of rockweed from tide pools or rocky parts of the beach. You can distinguish rockweed by the little bubbles or "poppers" in the strands. Be sure not to confuse it with kelp, Irish moss, or other common sea flora that you find along the shore, which don't react well to heat. Rinse the rockweed in seawater and keep it handy. You'll need it as you cook. You'll also need sturdy pot holders and at least one strong helper.

Now you want to get about eight to ten inches of seawater in the bottom of the "kettle." Have the aforementioned helper help you lug the can down to

At the Arlington House, near popular Nantasket Beach, Massachusetts, in the late nineteenth century, you could a get a seafood dinner for 50 cents, children under 10 half price.

the ocean. Try to wade out far enough to get clear, unsandy seawater. Lug it back, put it on the fire, and cover it till the water comes to a rolling boil.

Pile enough rockweed into the can to cover the bottom. Throw the foil-wrapped potatoes on top. Add more rockweed. Cover the can and let it steam/ boil for about twenty minutes. If you want to throw in some whole onions at this point, they give a nice flavor to everything and taste great.

Next come the lobsters. We use pound to pound-and-a-quarter "bugs" because they are plentiful and cheap in the high season here in New England, and they fit nicely on a standard plate. Throw in the lobsters and cover with more rockweed. Put the lid back on and steam for another twenty minutes or so.

Throw on the ears of corn in their green husks and cover with rockweed. Cook for fifteen minutes. Add clams, preferably tied in individual cheesecloth bags for ease of removal, and again add rockweed. Steam just until the clams open, another ten minutes or so. Throw out any broken or unopened clams. During this last step we melt a pound of butter in an old enamel pot at the edge of the fire.

When everything is ready—and the timing here is more art than science—use tongs

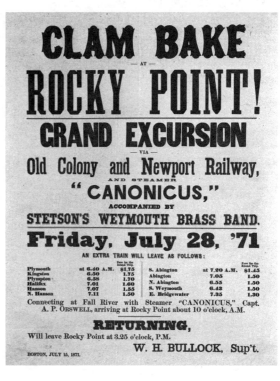

Complete with brass band, this excursion by "an extra train" and steamer culminated at a big clambake at Rocky Point, Rhode Island.

to decant everything into foil trays. You can also dump everything out onto a tarp, then have everyone grab a plate and dig in.

Our guests tend to eat on beach towels on the sand. Since the lobsters are often soft shells by mid- to late summer, they can usually be cracked by hand. Serve melted butter in disposable coffee cups for dipping clams and lobster, and for dribbling on the corn and potatoes. Knives and forks are available, but optional.

It will be obvious by this point that this is not a neat and tidy affair, nor is it low fat—unless you omit the butter, which is a mistake if you ask me. Nonetheless, I usually set out a bowl of lemon wedges.

In addition to the staples, I have been fortunate enough to have friends who bring all manner of wonderful things to accompany the feast, from sliced garden tomatoes to coleslaw, baguettes, and—last but not least—blueberry pie made from handpicked wild blueberries. It just doesn't get much better than this.

THE CLAM THAT ATE SEATTLE . . .

There are clams, and then there are geoducks (pronounced *gooey-ducks*)—one of the strangest and most grotesque bivalves known to humankind. Although their appearance is like a steamer clam, their size makes them look like something out of a 1950s sci-fi movie.

According to the Washington State Department of Ecology, geoducks:

- Range from 1 to 3 pounds, with a maximum recorded weight of 7.15 pounds.
- Can live to be more than 100 years old.
- Have siphons or necks than can extend to 39 inches.

It's estimated that there are some 109 million geoducks in Puget Sound. They are edible and are considered a delicacy in parts of Asia.

CLAMS ON THE HALF SHELL

I happen to prefer littlenecks, the smallest hard-shell clams for eating raw, but other people swear by the slightly larger cherrystones. Whatever your preference, when served on the half shell, the flesh should be a pale rosy color and should smell fresh and briny. As with oysters, it takes some practice to become adept at opening clams.

Rinse any sand or grit off the outside of the shell and allow the clams to rest for half an hour or so. If they are undisturbed, the shell seal may be a bit more relaxed.

Hold a clam in one hand, preferably using a heavy glove, and work a clam knife in between the shells opposite the hinged end. Once the knife is between the shells, turn it to pry them open. Use the knife to detach the clam from the top and bottom shells. Discard one of the shells and place the clam in the other to serve.

Like oysters, these can be served with Mignonette Sauce or a horseradish-and-ketchup-based Cocktail Sauce. (You'll find recipes for both in the Oysters chapter.) Serve with lemon wedges, allowing 6 clams per person as an hors d'oeuvre.

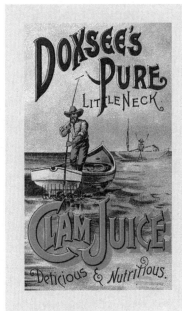

The clammer in the foreground on a trade card for Doxsee's Pure Little Neck Clam Juice is using a rake with a single long handle, while his compatriot in the background uses a double-handled tong.

BASIC STEAMED CLAMS

Soft-shell New England clams are often called steamers and—unlike cherrystones or littlenecks—are not eaten raw. They are, however, delicious when cooked. To eat the steamed clams, pull the clam from the shell by the black "neck" or siphon. There is a covering over this that you will need to pull off with a thumb and forefinger. Then swish the clam around in the broth as a last-minute rinse, dip the clam in butter, and eat it whole. Mahogany clams, littlenecks, and cherrystones can also be steamed, but for my money steamed clams are best with soft-shell clams.

3 pounds soft-shell or steamer
   clams
2 cups water, plus more as
   needed
1 teaspoon sea salt
2 cups white wine or beer, plus
   more as needed
4 tablespoons melted butter

1. Rinse the clams thoroughly to remove any grit or sand. Discard any that have broken shells.

2. Put the water, sea salt and wine or beer into a large, deep pot, adding more in equal parts until the liquid is 1 to 2 inches deep. Bring to a boil.

3. Add the steamers directly to the liquid, or put them in a steamer basket. Steam over high heat until the clams open, about 5 minutes. Discard any that do not open. Strain the broth into a small bowl.

4. Serve, adding a small bowl of broth and a little melted butter on the side for each person.

SERVES 6 AS AN APPETIZER

GRILLED LITTLENECK CLAMS WITH GARLIC AND PARSLEY

An Italian friend first served this wonderful dish to me. With people hanging around the grill, the clams never made it to the serving platter.

24 hard-shell littleneck or cherrystone clams
3 tablespoons butter
3 tablespoons extra-virgin
olive oil
1½ tablespoons finely chopped
Italian parsley
1½ tablespoons minced fresh
garlic
Lemon slices, for serving

1. Preheat a gas or charcoal grill. Rinse or scrub the clamshells till they're clean and free of sand and grit.

2. While the grill is heating, melt the butter and olive oil together in a small pan. Add the parsley and garlic, and sauté until the garlic is slightly translucent and fragrant, being careful not to brown it. Keep this mixture warm while you cook the clams.

3. Using a pair of tongs, place the clams on the grill and cook until they open. Using an oven mitt or heatproof glove, carefully twist the top shell off and place the full bottom shell back on the grill.

4. Spoon the garlic mixture over the clams and cook just until the mixture bubbles. Remove from the heat with tongs and serve with lemon slices.

Note: Depending on the size of the clams, the thickness of their shells, and the heat of the grill, they can take as long as 10 minutes to open but may begin to "pop" in as little as 2 minutes. Discard any that do not open.

SERVES 4 AS AN APPETIZER

CLAMS CASINO

According to Linda Beaulieu, author of *The Providence and Rhode Island Cookbook,* Clams Casino originated with "Julius Keller, maître d' in the original casino next to the seaside Towers in Narragansett." As with many classic dishes, there are numerous versions. This one uses quahogs, but you could use cherrystones if you prefer, doubling the number.

2 slices bacon

6 quahogs

3/4 cup water

3/4 cup white wine

1 tablespoon butter

3 tablespoons olive oil, divided

3/4 cup finely chopped onion

4 cloves garlic

1/2 cup finely chopped green peppers

1 cup Italian-style dried bread crumbs

1 tablespoon chopped fresh oregano

1/2 teaspoon red pepper flakes

1/2 cup grated Parmesan cheese

3 tablespoons of mayonnaise

2 tablespoons chopped flat-leaf parsley

Lemon wedges, for serving

1. Preheat the oven to 425°F.

2. In a large skillet, cook the bacon over medium heat until crisp. Remove the bacon, draining it on paper towels. Crumble into small pieces and reserve. Pour off all but 1 tablespoon of the bacon fat.

3. Wash the clams. Place them in a pot big enough to hold them with the water and wine. Steam until the clams open—about 10 to 15 minutes, depending on size. Discard any that do not open. When they're cool enough to handle, separate the shells and remove the meat, reserving the shells. Chop the clams coarsely and set aside.

4. Add the butter and 2 tablespoons of the oil to the skillet, and sauté the onion, garlic, and peppers until soft.

5. Add the bread crumbs, reserved bacon, oregano, red pepper flakes, cheese, mayonnaise, sautéed vegetables, and chopped clams. Mix well. Fill the clamshells with this mixture and place them on a baking sheet. Sprinkle with the parsley and drizzle with the remaining oil. Bake for 10 minutes or until hot and beginning to brown. Serve with lemon wedges.

SERVES 6 AS A FIRST COURSE

CLAMS WITH BLACK BEANS AND HAM
IN A CHINESE DARK WINE SAUCE

Arrows restaurant in Ogunquit, Maine, is widely recognized as one of the top dining establishments in New England. Chef-owners Clark Frasier and Mark Gaier recently opened a second restaurant in Ogunquit, which was an instant hit. Less formal than their original establishment, MC Perkins Cove features innovative dishes like this one.

3 tablespoons vegetable oil

4 ounces thinly sliced prosciutto, cut into strips

2 tablespoons finely chopped garlic

1 tablespoon finely chopped Chinese fermented black beans*

2 teaspoons chile paste*

2 cups chicken stock

1/2 cup Xian Xing wine* or dry red wine

1 tablespoons soy sauce

1 tablespoons rice vinegar

1 tablespoon finely chopped fresh ginger

36 small hard-shell clams, such as littlenecks, scrubbed clean

4 tablespoons unsalted butter

1 cup diced, peeled, seeded tomatoes

1 tablespoon Asian sesame oil

4 scallions, thinly sliced

* Items available at Asian specialty markets

1. In a large stainless-steel pot, warm the vegetable oil over medium heat. Add the prosciutto, garlic, beans, and chile paste and cook, stirring, for about 5 minutes. It's fine if these brown a bit. Add the chicken stock, wine, soy sauce, vinegar, and ginger, and bring to a boil. Use a wooden spoon to loosen the brown bits on the bottom. Reduce the heat to low and simmer for 15 minutes.

2. Increase the heat to high and return to a boil. Add the clams, cover, and cook, shaking the pot, until the clams open, about 2 minutes. Reduce the heat to medium. Using a slotted spoon, remove the clams and divide them among six warm soup plates or bowls.

3. Whisk the butter into the sauce a tablespoon at a time. Stir in the tomatoes and turn off the heat. Whisk in the sesame oil. Ladle the sauce on top of the clams. Sprinkle with the scallions and serve at once.

SERVES 6

SPAGHETTI WITH WHITE CLAM SAUCE

This Italian classic is a favorite in New England, too, especially in places like Boston's North End. It is simple to make but has a wonderful combination of flavors that really work well together.

4 dozen littleneck clams

1 cup water

3 tablespoons extra-virgin
olive oil

3 tablespoons butter

4 cloves garlic, minced

2 tablespoons chopped flat-leaf
parsley

1/2 cup dry white wine

Salt and pepper

1 pound dry linguini or spaghetti

1. Rinse the clams well under cold running water. In a large stockpot, steam the clams in the water until they open. When they're cool enough to handle, remove the meat from all but a dozen clams and chop coarsely. Strain the broth from the pan and reserve.

2. In a large skillet, heat the oil and add the butter. Cook over low heat till the butter is melted. Sauté the garlic until it's soft, about 3 minutes. Add the clam broth (you should have about 1½ cups), parsley, and wine, and simmer for about 5 minutes. Add the clam meat and simmer for another 3 minutes. Season to taste with salt and pepper. Cook spaghetti according to package directions.

3. Ladle over hot linguini or spaghetti and garnish each serving with three clams in the shell.

SERVES 4

This littoral scene depicts a clam shucking operation at Essex, Massachusetts, circa 1880.

MANHATTAN CLAM CHOWDER

Long spurned by New Englanders, this tomato-based chowder was likely created by immigrants of Mediterranean descent. Garlic and herbs give it a distinct and delicious flavor, reminiscent of the classic seafood stew, cioppino.

2 1/4-inch slices pancetta, diced

1 large onion, chopped

2 cloves garlic, minced

2 stalks celery, chopped

2 cups chopped (1/2 inch dice) peeled potatoes

1/2 cup chopped carrots

3 tablespoons flour

2 cups clam broth

2 cups Clamato® juice

2 cups tomato juice

2 tablespoons chopped fresh oregano

1 bay leaf

2 cups chopped clams, drained

1 tablespoon chopped Italian parsley

Olive oil, salt, black pepper, and hot sauce, to taste

Crusty bread, for serving

1. In a large pot or Dutch oven, fry the pancetta until it's crisp and its fat is rendered.

2. Add the onion, garlic, celery, potatoes, and carrots to the pot. Sauté for about 5 minutes.

3. Sprinkle the flour over the vegetables, stir to coat, and add the broth, Clamato® juice, and tomato juice. Bring to a boil, and continue boiling until the mixture begins to thicken.

4. Add the oregano and bay leaf, and simmer over low heat until the potatoes are soft, about 10 minutes.

5. Add the clams, parsley, and pancetta, and simmer for another 3 to 5 minutes. Remove bay leaf. Drizzle with a little olive oil, season to taste with salt, pepper, and hot sauce, and serve with crusty bread.

SERVES 8

NEW ENGLAND CLAM CHOWDER

This quintessential New England recipe has been around for many generations. In its original form it often used condensed milk, as fresh dairy was rarely available. This is a slightly updated version of the classic. I have made this using leftover steamer clams, but I prefer chopped hard-shell clams.

2 pounds cherrystone or little-
    neck clams

2 cups water

2 slices bacon, cut into 1-inch
    pieces

2 tablespoons butter, divided

1 cup chopped yellow onion

2 cups chopped (1/2-inch dice)
    potatoes

1 12-ounce can evaporated skim
    milk

1 cup half-and-half or light cream

1 teaspoon sea salt, or to taste

1 teaspoon white pepper

1/2 teaspoon Worcestershire
    sauce

Crackers, for serving

1. Rinse the clams thoroughly to remove any sand or grit from the out-side. Bring the water to a boil and add the clams. Steam until they open, about 5 to 7 minutes. Drain the clams into a bowl through a strainer lined with a several layers of cheesecloth or a coffee filter; reserve this broth. When the clams are cool enough to handle, remove them from their shells and chop coarsely. You should have at least 1/2 cup.

2. In a large pot, cook the bacon over medium heat until the fat is ren-dered and the bacon is crisp. Remove from the pot and drain on paper towels. Crumble or chop finely. Drain bacon fat off.

3. Melt 1 tablespoon of the butter in the pot and add the onion. Sauté for about 3 minutes until soft. Add the potatoes and stir to coat with melted butter. Cook for another 2 minutes over medium heat.

4. Add 1 1/2 cups of the reserved clam broth and simmer until the pota-toes are soft but not mushy, about 10 to 12 minutes. Add the clams and bacon and simmer for another 3 minutes.

5. Add the evaporated milk and half-and-half or light cream. Add the salt, pepper, and Worcestershire and stir to blend. Heat thoroughly but do not boil. Float the remaining tablespoon of butter on top. Serve hot with crackers.

MAKES 5 SERVINGS, 1 CUP EACH

FLO'S RHODE ISLAND CLAM CHOWDER

Just down the road from Mystic Seaport is a tiny breakfast-and-lunch restaurant by the name of Kitchen Little. It's well known for its Rhode Island Clam Chowder, a clear-broth chowder that leaves out the milk and cream. Being a northern New Englander, I was skeptical at first, but it is absolutely delicious—and less caloric than the standard New England Clam Chowder.

1 quart unopened quahogs

1 large onion, diced

6 tablespoons bacon grease

4 large red potatoes, diced

1 8-ounce jar of clam broth

½ teaspoon white pepper

1 tablespoon chopped fresh basil

Crackers, for serving

1. In a large pot or Dutch oven, bring an inch or two of water to a boil. Add the quahogs and steam until the clams have opened. When the clams are cool enough to handle, remove the meat and chop coarsely. Strain the broth from the pot and set aside.

2. Sauté the onion in the bacon grease until soft, about 3 minutes. Add the potatoes and all the clam broth to cover.

3. Bring to a boil and simmer over low heat until the potatoes are tender but not mushy, about 8 minutes. Add the clam meat and simmer for 2 minutes. Remove from the heat and stir in the pepper and basil. Serve hot with crackers.

SERVES 6

THE THREE CHOWDERS

It's generally thought that the word chowder derives from the French word *chaudiere,* or "cauldron," referring to the pot in which coastal French fishermen made their fish soups. And though chowders may share this common ancestor, a debate has long raged in the northeastern United States about what constitutes a proper clam chowder.

Northern New Englanders swear by milk- or cream-based chowders, insisting that anything else is an impostor. The classic Manhattan Clam Chowder uses no dairy and is tomato based. What is known as Rhode Island Clam Chowder takes a middle ground by using neither dairy nor tomatoes, but simplifying matters to clams, broth, onions, and potatoes. And although I risk getting drummed out of my hometown in Maine by saying so, all three can be excellent.

"And the mussel pooled and heron
Priested shore . . ."

—DYLAN THOMAS, *POEM IN OCTOBER*

Mussels

Until relatively recently Americans have regarded mussels as the poor relations in the shellfish family. Although the colonists came from mussel-eating places in England and Europe, they didn't eat American mussels, possibly on the advice of Native Americans who may have shunned them due to red tide risk. Not much had changed by the late nineteenth century when Fannie Farmer described mussels as an inferior sort of oyster and didn't even provide a recipe for them in her 1896 *Boston Cooking School Cookbook*.

In Europe mussels have always gotten more respect. Blue mussels have been cultivated there since medieval times and have been a food source since time immemorial. *Moules et frites* (mussels and french fries) is practically the national dish of Belgium, usually accompanied by a strong Belgian beer. In the 1970s the French alone were consuming nearly thirty times more mussels than Americans. Now Americans are consuming ten times as many mussels as we did in the 1970s. We haven't caught up with the Europeans yet, but we're gaining.

In this country mussels are cultivated on ropes and stakes. In New England wild mussels are dragged up from the sea bottom. Some musseling operations drag up small seed mussels and replant them on leased beds until the mussels reach marketable size. After the wild mussels are harvested, they are placed in saltwater tanks until they have purged themselves; then they're cleaned, graded, and sent to market.

The blue mussel is by far the most common in the United States, but the larger green mussel, usually imported from New Zealand, is gaining some in popularity.

It's easy to gather mussels yourself—easier than clamming or oystering—but there are a few things to keep in mind. Mussels should come from clean, open water at or below the low-tide mark, so you're going to have to get your feet wet. The mussels will be attached to rocks or pilings and will need to be well rinsed and scrubbed before you cook them.

In the waters around Mystic Seaport, for instance, there are hard clams (quahogs), scallops, and some mussels, but as with many coastal areas, the shoreside development and the narrow inlets of the nearby harbors mean that much of the area is often closed to shellfishing.

An early aquaculturist grows mussels on ropes that are suspended in saltwater.

HOW TO PREPARE
MUSSELS FOR COOKING

The rope-grown farmed mussels available in the fish section of many supermarkets are wonderfully clean and often need less preparation than wild-gathered mussels, but you should still rinse and "debeard" them. The "beard" is the fibrous material that mussels use to attach themselves to the ropes, piers, rocks, or pilings on which they are growing. To remove it, feel the straighter side of the shell where the mussel is hinged. Grab any fibers between your thumb and forefinger and pull firmly. Use a small pair of pliers if you need to. Discard the beard and any mussels that gape open.

If you are using mussels you have gathered yourself, be prepared to rinse them thoroughly in several changes of seawater and, if possible, let them soak for a couple of hours to rid themselves of any grit. Scrub the shells with a stiff brush and scrape off any barnacles, then debeard as above.

Sea Silk

The mussel's beard has long been woven into fabric. Ancient Greek fishermen used gloves woven of these fibers (called *byssus*) that were so durable, the gloves were handed down from generation to generation. Byssus cloth was being woven in Italy as late as the 1920s.

MUSSELS STEAMED IN WHITE WINE

This is similar to one of the simplest, most classic mussel preparations—the French *moules mariniere*—but uses garlic instead of shallots.

1 cup dry white wine

3 cloves garlic, minced

1 tablespoon extra-virgin olive oil

4 dozen mussels, cleaned and
    debearded

Lemon slices, for serving

1 small baguette, sliced, for
    soaking up cooking liquid

1. Combine the wine, garlic, and olive oil in a saucepan.

2. Bring to a low boil and add the mussels.

3. Turn the heat down so that the liquid is simmering and cook until the mussels open wide enough to see the meat inside, 3 to 5 minutes. Discard any mussels that do not open.

4. Serve hot in bowls with lemon slices and sliced bread.

SERVES 4 AS AN APPETIZER

MOLLY MALONE

In Dublin's fair city,

Where the girls are so pretty

I first set my eyes on sweet Molly Malone

As she wheeled her wheel barrow

Thro' streets broad and narrow

Crying "Cockles and Mussels alive, alive O

Alive, alive O! Alive, alive O"

Crying "Cockles and Mussels alive, alive O."

MUSSELS FRA DIAVOLO

This recipe is based on the classic Italian preparation. Once again, a loaf of good crusty bread is mandatory for sopping up the delicious pan juices. You could also serve this over linguini or spaghetti.

2½ tablespoons extra-virgin
  olive oil, divided
2 shallots, chopped
4 cloves garlic, minced
1 cup good-quality canned Italian
  plum tomatoes, coarsely
  chopped
2 tablespoons chopped fresh
  oregano
1 cup white vermouth
½ teaspoon hot red pepper
  flakes, or to taste
2 pounds mussels, cleaned and
  debearded
Crusty bread, for serving

1. Heat 1½ tablespoons of the olive oil in a Dutch oven or large sauté pan. Add the shallots and sauté until soft.

2. Add the garlic, tomatoes, oregano, and vermouth, and simmer gently for 5 minutes. Add the red pepper flakes and stir.

3. Add the mussels and cover. Cook until the mussels are fully open, about 5 to 7 minutes. Discard any that do not open.

4. Drizzle the remaining tablespoon of olive oil over the mussels. Ladle the mussels into four small bowls, and ladle the remaining pan juices over them. Serve with warm crusty bread.

SERVES 4

SPICY THAI MUSSELS

This Asian-influenced recipe reflects the Thai culinary tradition of balancing different types of flavors, such as lemon grass, coconut, and chili sauce for a completely delicious outcome.

½ tablespoon butter

½ tablespoon olive oil

2–3 shallots, chopped

3 cloves garlic, peeled and sliced, divided

1 14-ounce can whole tomatoes

2 stalks lemongrass, outside stalk removed, white base sliced lengthwise then into 1-inch pieces

1 pint (2 cups) coconut milk

2 teaspoons chili garlic sauce (more to taste)

1 cup white wine

1 cup clam juice

2 pounds mussels, cleaned and debearded

2–3 scallions, split lengthwise and then cut into 2-inch pieces.

1 tablespoon chopped cilantro

1. In a medium-size saucepan, heat the butter and olive oil over low heat. Sauté the shallots until translucent, about 3 minutes. Add 1 tablespoon of the garlic and sauté until soft.

2. Add the tomatoes to the pan reserving the juice, crushing them with the back of a wooden spoon. Add the lemongrass.

3. Add the coconut milk and chili garlic sauce and let the mixture simmer over low heat until slightly thickened, 3 to 5 minutes. If the sauce seems too thick, add some of the tomato juice. You can prepare the recipe up to this stage and then refrigerate it for up to 2 days, if you like.

4. In a large pot, bring the wine, clam juice, and remaining garlic to a boil. Add the mussels and cook until they open.

5. Drain the mussels, discarding any that didn't open. Put them into a large, shallow serving bowl. Heat the cream sauce and stir in the scallions and cilantro. Pour over the mussels. Serve immediately.

SERVES 4

BROILED MUSSELS WITH PARSLEY-ARTICHOKE PESTO

This is a great appetizer for a dinner party when having everyone dive into a big bowl of mussels with their hands could get a little too messy. It would also make a great party hors d'oeuvre. Any leftover pesto can be frozen. You can also serve it over pasta, or spread it on French bread and broil until bubbling hot.

1 cup chopped flat-leaf or Italian parsley
3/4 cup grated Parmesan cheese
1/3 cup mayonnaise
1 14-ounce can artichoke hearts, drained
1/3 cup olive oil
Hot sauce, to taste
1/2 cup water
1/2 cup white wine
2 pounds mussels, cleaned and debearded
Lemon slices, for serving

1. Combine the parsley, Parmesan, mayonnaise, artichoke hearts, olive oil, and hot sauce in a food processor. Process until well combined.

2. Bring the water and wine to a boil in a medium saucepan. Add the mussels and steam, covered, until they open—3 to 5 minutes. Discard any unopened mussels.

3. Drain the mussels. When they're cool enough to handle, remove one shell and loosen the mussel meat from the other. Place the mussels in their shells on a baking sheet covered with crumpled aluminum foil to keep them level.

4. Spoon about a teaspoon of the pesto on top of each mussel and broil until bubbling and hot, about a minute. Serve with lemon slices. Any leftover pesto or mussels would be great over pasta, or on flatbread.

SERVES 4 AS AN APPETIZER

"Sometimes, when I am out foraging the seashore at low tide, I become so interested in the pursuit of scallops that I forget to go in for my lunch, but I don't grow hungry. I just open a few scallops on the spot and eat their sweet muscles with no sauce but their own juicy, sea-given saltiness."

—EUELL GIBBONS, *STALKING THE BLUE EYED SCALLOP*

Scallops

When I got married in 1987, my husband and I had invited, among other friends, a local fisherman, known for his reticence as well as his fishing skills. He did not come to the wedding but four months later, shortly before Christmas, he appeared on our doorstep with what was surely the most mouthwatering gift we received—a full two pounds of sea scallops, freshly caught just a few miles from our house, cleaned and delivered within hours of being on the seafloor. I'll take that over a candy dish any day.

Lobstermen in our part of New England have in previous years turned to scalloping during the winter months, when scallops are in season and lobsters aren't. There is no expensive gear to be lost in winter storms, traps needn't be hauled and rebaited, and scallop prices are usually high enough to make it worthwhile. But it's hard work, nonetheless.

There are two primary types of scallops consumed in this country: bay scallops and sea scallops. Each type has its own following, but I prefer the larger and whiter sea scallops. Since scallops are prone to drying out, the larger type allows more time for searing, browning, or frying, without turning the scallops to rubber, which is easily done with overcooking. You can expect from twenty to forty sea scallops per pound and about fifty to ninety bay scallops.

Unlike most of the other bivalves we eat here in the United States, we consume only the large adductor muscle of the scallop, which is the muscle that opens and closes the shell. In Europe scallops are cooked whole, including the roe, which turns a dull orange color when cooked. The adductor muscle is especially well developed in scallops, unlike other bivalves, as scallops can actually "swim." Unlike their stationary cousins, such as clams, mussels, and oysters, scallops can open and close their shells to propel themselves through the water. Some scallops wander farther afield than others, but all are capable of movement.

Scallops are either dredged from the ocean floor or caught by divers. "Diver" and "dayboat" scallops are more prized, as they tend to be less battered in the harvesting; they're also taken ashore—and thus to market—sooner. You may see scallops in the market that are labeled as "dry," and while intuitively this seems like a bad thing, "dry" scallops are preferable to scallops that have had moisture added to them to compensate for moisture loss after harvest. The dry scallops are more expensive per pound, but they are well worth the price. You know you are getting a fresher product, and you're not paying for the extra brine that has been added.

Until the early 1900s scallops were not highly valued and seemed as much a source of culinary confusion as anything else. Even in France, where a greater variety of ingredients has been used for a longer time, it wasn't until the twentieth century that coquilles Saint-Jacques became popular. Even this is a bit confusing to Americans: In France the term *coquilles Saint-Jacques* refers not only to the scallops themselves as an ingredient but also a way of preparing them.

These days scallops appear in dozens of preparations everywhere from your local fish shack to Michelin-starred restaurants. Good scallops smell like fresh sea air, briny but slightly sweet, and have a taste that's almost as delicate.

BROILED SCALLOPS IN PROSCIUTTO

This is a slightly more sophisticated take on the classic scallops-in-bacon hors d'oeuvre. It's delicious with a chilled Prosecco, an Italian sparkling wine.

¼ cup horseradish mustard

12 thin slices of prosciutto, halved lengthwise into long strips

1 dozen sea scallops, halved

1 lemon, cut into wedges, for serving

1. Preheat the broiler.

2. Spread a little of the mustard on each piece of prosciutto.

3. Wrap each scallop in a strip of prosciutto and secure with a small skewer or toothpick. Broil the scallops until just cooked through, about 3 to 5 minutes. Serve hot with lemon wedges.

SERVES 6 AS AN HORS D'OEUVRE

DAVE K.'S SCALLOP CASSEROLE

Both of the lobstermen I know who scallop in winter prepare their scallops only one way. This simple preparation lets the sweetness and freshness of the scallops really shine through.

1 pound sea scallops

3 tablespoons butter, divided

2 teaspoons fresh lemon juice, divided

Salt and pepper, to taste

1 cup crushed Ritz crackers

1. Preheat the oven to 450°F. Pat the scallops dry and cut them in half if they are very large.

2. Place half the butter in a casserole dish, and put it into the oven until the butter has melted. Remove the pan from the oven and add the scallops, half the lemon juice, and salt and pepper.

3. Melt the remaining butter in a small bowl or pan; mix in the cracker crumbs and remaining lemon juice until well blended. Cover the scallops with this mixture. Bake for 15 to 20 minutes, or until the scallops are just cooked through and the topping is golden brown.

SERVES 2-4

ESCALLOPED SCALLOPS

In *Old Boston Fare in Food and Pictures,* historian and chef Jerome Rubin chronicled the culinary life of Boston in a photographic history of New England's largest city and her people. The technique of "escalloping" is a classic preparation that usually involves cooking in a cream sauce and baking with a crumb topping. This is an adaptation of Rubin's recipe for this traditional New England dish.

1½ pints (3 cups) scallops

1 cup white wine

1 pound mushrooms, sliced

1 green pepper, coarsely chopped

1 small onion, finely chopped

4 tablespoons butter, divided

2 tablespoons flour

1 cup cream or whole milk

Buttered bread crumbs

¼ teaspoon paprika

1. Preheat the oven to 400°F.

2. Poach the scallops in the wine for 3 minutes and reserve the liquid. Drain, cool, and cut the scallops in half horizontally.

3. Sauté the mushrooms, green pepper, and onion in 2 tablespoons of the butter until soft.

4. Make a white sauce by melting the remaining butter in a saucepan. When it's melted, whisk in the flour and cook over low heat for 2 minutes. Gradually whisk in the cream or milk and the reserved scallop liquid.

5. Gently combine the scallops, vegetables, and sauce in a casserole dish. Top with the bread crumbs and paprika, and bake for 10 to 12 minutes or until golden brown and bubbling.

SERVES 4

MAINE SHRIMP AND SCALLOP CEVICHE

I first had ceviche (pronounced *sah-VEE-chay*) in Key West, Florida, with a combination of seafood including conch. I think this method lends itself very well to New England shellfish such as scallops and shrimp. Maine native shrimp are small, tender, and seasonal, available in early spring. The citrus, salt, and peppers "cook" the shrimp and scallops until they are opaque and flavorful.

½ cup lime juice

¼ cup orange juice

¼ cup minced red bell pepper

1 poblano chile, minced (or jalapeño, if you like a little more heat)

1 shallot, minced

2 tablespoons chopped fresh cilantro

1 teaspoon grated fresh ginger

1 tablespoon sea salt

½ pound native Maine shrimp or other small shrimp, peeled but uncooked

1 pound sea scallops, cut into quarters

Lime wedges, for serving

1. In a large glass or ceramic bowl, combine all the ingredients except the shrimp, scallops, and lime wedges.

2. Add the shrimp and scallops. Toss well to coat.

3. Refrigerate for 6 hours or more, until the shrimp and scallops are opaque and have absorbed the flavors of the marinade.

4. Serve cold in small bowls with a wedge of lime.

SERVES 6 AS A FIRST COURSE

Sorting scallops aboard the research vessel *Delaware* in 1961.

NANTUCKET SCALLOP CHOWDER

This dish is adapted from Imogene Wolcott's recipe in *The New England Yankee Cookbook*, first published in 1939. She suggests removing the onions after they are sautéed, but leaving them in creates a more flavorful chowder.

4 tablespoons butter

2 small onions, sliced

1 cup peeled and diced potatoes

1 cup white wine or white
    vermouth

1 cup water

1 pint (2 cups) scallops, cut into
    ½-inch pieces

4 cups hot milk

Sea salt and white pepper,
    to taste

Crackers, for serving

1. In a large saucepan, melt the butter over low heat. Sauté the onions until soft and golden.

2. Add the potatoes to the pan, add wine or vermouth and water, and bring to a boil. Simmer for 20 minutes.

3. Add this mixture to the scallops and simmer gently for 10 minutes.

4. Add hot milk; season to taste with salt and white pepper. Serve immediately with crackers.

Note: If you prefer a smoother bisque consistency, puree half the chowder in a food processor or blender and add back to the remaining chowder, mixing well.

SERVES 6

SCALLOPS NANTUCKET

The Captain Daniel Packer Inne in Mystic, Connecticut, is a local landmark. Built in 1756, the inn now serves some of the best food in the area, with original preparations of classic New England dishes. This is the chef's tribute to Nantucket scallops.

FOR THE HERB BUTTER

8 tablespoons salted butter, softened

1 teaspoon fresh garlic

Pinch of thyme

1/2 teaspoon chopped rosemary

1 teaspoon Dijon mustard

Salt and pepper, to taste

FOR THE SCALLOPS

2 pounds sea scallops

1/2 cup white wine

1/4 cup fresh lemon juice

1/2 pound mild cheddar, thinly sliced

1 cup panko (Japanese bread crumbs)

1. Preheat the oven to 375°F.

2. Make the Herb Butter: Mix all the ingredients together until well blended.

3. Make the Scallops: Divide the scallops into four to six portions and put them into individual casseroles or ramekins.

4. Pour a splash of white wine and lemon juice over each serving. Add a tablespoon of Herb Butter to each, then lay two thin slices of cheddar atop. Sprinkle the panko over everything and bake for 13 to 15 minutes.

SERVES 4-6

The whole, opened scallop. Americans only eat the adductor muscle (upper left) while others around the world eat the whole creature.

BAKED SEA SCALLOPS IN APPLE SOUR CREAM SAUCE

Chefs James Haller and Jeffrey Paige developed this delicious recipe for scallops while cooking at the Shaker Table restaurant in Canterbury, New Hampshire. It appears in the new edition of their book *Cooking in the Shaker Spirit*.

FOR THE SAUCE

2 tablespoons unsalted butter

2 tablespoons minced shallots

3 tablespoons flour

1/4 cup white wine

1 tablespoon Dijon mustard

1/2 cup apple juice concentrate

1 1/2 cups sour cream

Salt and pepper, to taste

FOR THE SCALLOPS

2 pounds sea scallops

1 tablespoon unsalted butter plus
    more for the pan

1 cup bread crumbs

1. Make the Sauce: Melt the butter in a saucepan and sauté the shallots until soft. Add the flour to the butter and whisk to make a smooth roux. Add the wine, mustard, and apple juice concentrate, stirring until smooth.

2. Add the sour cream and cook over very low heat for 10 to 15 minutes. Season to taste with salt and pepper.

3. Preheat the oven to 400°F.

4. Make the Scallops: Place the sea scallops in a well-buttered baking dish and pour the Apple Sour Cream Sauce over the top.

5. Melt the butter in the pan and mix in the bread crumbs. Sprinkle the crumbs over the scallops and bake for 30 minutes or until bubbly and light brown.

SERVES 6

SEARED SCALLOPS

WITH ROASTED GARLIC AND YELLOW PEPPER SAUCE

This may seem like a lot of garlic, but when it's roasted, garlic has a sweet nutty flavor that enhances the natural sweetness of scallops.

1 head garlic

1 teaspoon olive oil

2 yellow bell peppers

1 shallot, minced

1 tablespoon fresh lemon juice

1/2 cup chicken or seafood stock

2 tablespoons flour

1 teaspoon salt

1/2 teaspoon white pepper

2 teaspoons peanut oil

20 sea scallops

1. Preheat the oven to 350°F.

2. Peel the loose outer skin from the garlic and cut off the pointed end of the head so the top of each clove is exposed. Drizzle with the olive oil and wrap in foil, cut-end up. Bake the head until it's completely soft and golden and the cloves can be squeezed out, about 40 minutes. When cool enough to handle, squeeze the cloves into a bowl and set aside.

3. Broil the peppers whole, turning until each side is black and blistered and peppers are soft. Remove from the heat and let cool, wrapped loosely in paper towels or a brown paper bag. When the peppers are cool enough to handle, peel off the blackened skin, remove the seeds and membranes inside, and chop coarsely.

4. Combine the roasted garlic, peppers, shallot, lemon juice, and stock in a food processor and blend until smooth.

5. Mix the flour, salt, and pepper together in a shallow bowl. Heat the peanut oil in a frying pan over high heat. Quickly roll the scallops in the flour mixture until they're lightly coated, shaking off any excess.

6. Sear the scallops in the frying pan (preferably cast iron or heavy non-stick) until both top and bottom are nicely browned. Serve immediately over the Roasted Garlic and Yellow Pepper Sauce.

SERVES 4

PART TWO
MEET THE CRUSTACEANS

"The sweet, salty, sensual delight of a claw dipped into drawn butter more than compensates for the lobster's cockroachlike appearance."

—LINDA GREENLAW, *THE LOBSTER CHRONICLES*

Lobster

Boiled lobster, broiled lobster, lobster bisque, lobster rolls—lobster in all its forms—may well be the most prized delicacy to come from New England's chilly ocean waters. But this wasn't always the case. The history of lobster fishing is a rags-to-riches story.

If you were a young boy walking along the shore in a town like Mystic, Connecticut, in the 1700s, you might well find a five- or even a ten-pound lobster just by looking among the rocks. You could feed a good-size family on just one of these giants, but you probably wouldn't even bother to pick it up unless your family was short of food or money. Prosperous people just didn't eat lobsters. Back then lobsters were so plentiful that they were fed to prisoners and indentured servants in lieu of more valuable foods such as cod or mackerel. Small lobsters—those less than a couple of pounds—weren't considered worth the bother and were often dumped onto fields as fertilizer.

According to Colin Woodard in his book *The Lobster Coast*, coastal New Englanders had been catching and eating lobster since the 1600s, but no one had ever tried to establish a commercial, moneymaking enterprise from these crustaceans.

So how did lobster become such a prized commodity and such a culinary superstar? As always, the law of supply and demand can alter the course of just about anything. When lobsters were so abundant, they weren't worth much, but as they became recognized as a cheap and plentiful foodstuff, especially for feeding the increasing number of immigrant laborers who landed on the East Coast in the 1800s, a fishery grew up.

A prize specimen in Noank, Connecticut, circa 1930.

When the easy-to-catch tide pool lobsters became scarce, people started to fish from rowboats near the shore. But this couldn't meet the increasing demand from cities like New York. The sailing "lobster smack" was designed by New London fishermen to solve this logistical problem. Smacks had large tanks built into them. Salt water circulated freely through the tank, keeping a cargo of lobsters fresh for up to a week on their journey to the markets in New York City.

Mystic Seaport's *Estella A.*, built in 1904, is an example of a sailboat built to fish for lobsters. In the next few decades, though, lobstermen began the switch to engine power, and many lobster smacks were abandoned. Some that had auxiliary power, like the *Estella A.*, were converted for use as pleasure boats.

Mystic Seaport's lobster sloop *Estella A.* She is of the type often referred to as a Friendship sloop.

But it wasn't till the later 1800s that lobsters began to get some real respect. During Victorian times New Englanders romanticized the lives of the earliest settlers, promoting the pleasant but fictional idea that our forefathers were taught how to create seaside feasts by local Native Americans. There's no evidence of this, although the coastal tribes were great shellfish eaters (as plentiful shell middens along the coast attest). Nonetheless, clambakes and shore picnics became hugely popular summer celebrations, with menus that included clams, chowder, lobster, potatoes, onions, breads, pies, and ripe watermelon—all the bounties of the season.

Lobsters became scarcer and more difficult to fish for as the demand increased. The rest, as they say, is history.

The familiarity that bred such contempt in colonial times is long gone, and the New England lobster industry is now highly regulated and very lucrative—if volatile. The investment required to enter the field is daunting. A far cry from gathering five-pound lobsters in tide pools, fishermen or -women now must invest in a boat, gear, licensing fees, insurance, and dockage, as well as find the best way to get their catch to market, often through a wholesaler or cooperative. The cost of entry to the fishery can run to $100,000 or more.

Lobster fishing boats of Bristol, Maine, hauling lobster traps in the days before powered boats and powered winches.

The size of lobsters that can be legally taken is strictly regulated. To be of legal size, a lobster's carapace or thorax must be at least 3¼ inches long. Female lobsters carrying fertilized eggs are also off-limits. You can tell a female lobster from a male by the tiny fins or "swimmerettes" on the underside of the lobster's tail. The males have rigid ones, while the females' are flexible and fanlike.

When buying lobster, always look for lively specimens that wave their claws and snap their tails. These will keep in the refrigerator covered with a damp cloth or newspaper for twenty-four hours or so, but it's best to buy them as close to the time you're going to cook them as possible.

While traditional lobster preparations remain deservedly popular, lobsters are now finding their way into modern haute cuisine—as you will see in some of the recipes that follow.

BASIC BOILED LOBSTER

Boiling a lobster is one of the easiest things you can do in the kitchen. All you have to do is watch your timer and make sure the lobsters are bright red when you remove them from the pot. If you are lucky enough to be near clean ocean water, by all means use it to boil your lobster.

6 quarts water

½ cup sea salt

4 lively lobsters, 1¼–1½ pounds each

1 lemon, cut into 4 wedges, for serving

6 tablespoons melted butter, for serving

1. Bring the water and salt to a boil in a pot large enough to also accommodate the lobsters with ease.

2. Plunge the lobsters into the boiling water headfirst and cover.

3. Boil for 12 minutes.

4. Remove the lobsters from the pot and rinse them briefly in cool water.

5. Serve immediately with lemon wedges and/or melted butter.

To steam lobsters, bring 4 inches of salted water to a boil in the bottom of a large pot and add lobsters headfirst. Steam for 15 minutes.

Note: If you want to make it easier for your guests to remove the meat from the shell, you can split the tail lengthwise and crack the claws with a nutcracker or heavy knife. If the lobsters are soft shell, it's often possible just to crack the shells by hand.

SERVES 4

LOBSTER BYTE

As a lobster grows, it sheds its shell, increasing in weight by 25 percent each time, and a lobster will shed its shell as many as twenty-four times in the first years of its life.

—Courtesy of the Maine Lobster Promotion Council

LOBSTER ROLLS

There are many versions of lobster rolls and lobster salad throughout New England. This one is simple, and the taste of the lobster really shines through. If you want something a little fancier, you can serve it on a croissant or baguette, but grilled hot dog rolls are classic.

2 lobsters (1 pound each),
    cooked and shelled; or
    $1/2$ pound fresh lobster meat,
    chopped
2 tablespoons good mayonnaise
1 teaspoon minced celery
1 teaspoon minced onion
$1/4$ teaspoon Old Bay Seasoning
Butter
2 split-top hot dog rolls

1. Boil the lobsters; when they're cool enough to handle, remove the meat and chop it coarsely. It should still be slightly warm.
2. Mix the warm meat with the mayonnaise, celery, onion, and seasoning in a bowl. Refrigerate until you're ready to fill the rolls.
3. Butter the sides of the split-top hot dog rolls. Grill each side in a frying pan until just golden.
4. Fill the rolls and serve.

SERVES 2

LOBSTER SOOP

This recipe for "soop" (sic) appeared in the *Compleat American Housewife,* first published in 1787.

"Boil the knuckle of veal to a jelly—strain it off—and season it as you please, put to it the body and tails of 3 lobsters a pint of white wine—make balls of the claws finely beaten and the yolks of 2 eggs, nutmeg, pepper and salt—boil them—and then fry them in butter and put them in ye soop."

HOW TO EAT A LOBSTER
AND MAINTAIN YOUR DIGNITY

No one was born knowing how to eat a lobster, although some crusty New England types might try to give you that impression.

There are two types of lobster eaters: those who pride themselves on getting every last little bit of edible meat out the critter and those who confine themselves to the big parts and don't venture in those suspect areas with odd, unidentifiable bits.

No matter which kind of lobster eater you aspire to be, everyone begins the same way: with the claws and the tail. The claws are the easiest to get at: Take the lobster cracker (a seagoing nutcracker, actually) and crack the claw through the thickest section. If you are unlucky, the claw will squirt precious lobster juice all over your shirt. (If you have succumbed to the total ignominy of having the waitress tie one of those plastic bibs on you at the beginning of the meal, you won't get lobster juice all over your shirt but you will look even more foolish. Far better to wear the scars of battle on your shirtfront than look like a hugely overgrown two-year-old throughout the entire meal.)

But to return to the claw: Crack it with the crackers and pull the meat out with the fork provided or the lobster pick, which resembles an oversized dental instrument. Dunk the meat in melted butter (having acquired a note from your doctor) and pop it into your mouth.

The knuckles between the claws and the body also contain useful amounts of meat but are harder going than the tail, so let's move on to the tail.

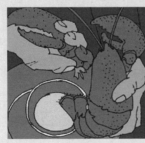  

Grasp the body in one hand and the tail in the other, and twist as if you really mean it. The tail will come away from the body. At the juncture of the tail and the body is some stuff that I believe is best ignored: The good stuff is still inside the tail. At this point, the more refined will take a knife and slit lengthwise the underside of the tail and pull the meat out. The less refined will break off the end of the tail, stick in their index finger and push the meat out. For obvious reasons, this is a technique more often seen at picnic tables than banquet tables. The tail meat is naturally divided lengthwise in half. I suggest you pull out the dark strip in the middle. (This is a harmless intestine of sorts, but I don't need to dwell on that.)

The little fins at the end of the tail often have a bit of meat in them as well as some sweet juice. Break off the fins, place one between your teeth, and squeeze the meat out. This tooth-strainer also works well for the eight little legs on the each side of the body.

At the big end of the tail, you're going to find some unusual looking "stuff," including the "green stuff" called tomalley, which is the lobster's liver. Some love it, some caution that this is where any pollutants in the lobster would be concentrated.

The "red stuff" is unfertilized eggs called "coral"—probably only by the lobster marketing board. At one time the eggs were considered a delicacy like caviar, but I think the only similarity is that they are both fishy eggs, although my co-author and I disagree on this point.

In the body cavity are some little bits of meat. It's easy to tell what's edible and what isn't. When in doubt, it probably isn't.

And if all else fails, just look for advice under your plate. Nearly every self-respecting lobster joint uses the same placemat "How to Eat a Lobster."

—Artwork courtesy of the Gulf of Maine Aquarium

SEAMEN'S INNE CREAMY LOBSTER BISQUE

The Seamen's Inne—on the grounds of Mystic Seaport—is a year-round restaurant with an 1800s ambience. A meal in its elegant dining room or cozy tavern makes a great end to any visit to the Seaport. Although there are many versions of lobster bisque, the inn's is one of my favorites.

This recipe calls for either lobster base—a concentrated soup base much like bouillon—or Lobster Stock. If you're using the latter, see the recipe that follows.

½ cup butter

1 medium onion, finely diced

½ cup celery, finely diced

1 teaspoon minced garlic

Pinch of thyme

¼ teaspoon paprika

¼ cup flour

½ cup plus 2 tablespoons sherry,
   divided

½ cup tomato juice

1 tablespoon lobster base plus
   3 cups water; or
   3 cups Lobster Stock

Hot sauce, sea salt, and pepper,
   to taste

1 cup heavy cream

1 bay leaf

1. Melt the butter in a large pot or Dutch oven over low heat. Sauté the onion, celery, and garlic until soft. Add the thyme and paprika and cook for 1 to 2 minutes more.

2. Stir in the flour a little at a time until you have a roux or thin paste. Cook for 4 to 5 minutes, stirring frequently. Whisk in ½ cup of the sherry and cook for 1 minute more.

3. Whisk in the tomato juice along with lobster base and water or Lobster Stock. Add bay leaf and simmer until the mixture begins to thicken, stirring constantly.

4. Season with hot sauce, sea salt, and pepper, if desired. Simmer for another 5 minutes.

5. Stir in the heavy cream and remaining 2 tablespoons of sherry. Reduce the heat to less than a simmer and stir until the soup is piping hot.

SERVES 6

LOBSTER BYTE

A lobster's age is approximately its weight multiplied by four, plus three years.

—Courtesy of the Maine Lobster Promotion Council

LOBSTER STOCK

Lobster stock is a key ingredient for lobster bisque and other lobster sauces, but you can also use it to create pasta sauces, to poach fish, and as a shellfish soup base. It freezes well and is a great way to make use of leftover cooked lobsters or shells. There are many versions of this recipe; this is how I like to make mine.

3 lobsters, 1 pound each, or 8 bodies and shells

1/2 cup butter

1/3 cup dark rum or brandy

1/2 cup chopped leeks

1/2 cup chopped celery

1/4 cup chopped shallots

1/4 cup chopped carrots

1 cup dry white wine

1 tablespoon fresh or dried herbs, such as tarragon, thyme, or chives

3 cups lobster cooking liquid or 1 1/2 cups water and 1 1/2 cups chicken stock (approximate)

1/3 cup tomato paste

1. If you are starting with live lobsters, boil them until just barely cooked through, 6 to 8 minutes. Drain, retaining the cooking liquid. Remove the meat over a bowl and reserve both juice and meat. If you are starting with shells, pick any remaining meat out of the bodies and shells and set aside. Break or chop the shells into 1- to 2-inch pieces.

2. Melt the butter in a large stockpot. Take a handful of the shells and sauté them over low heat for 5 minutes, being sure not to burn the butter. Carefully add the rum or brandy and—tipping the pan away from you slightly—touch a match to the liquid. Flambé until the flames subside.

3. Add the remaining shells, lobster bodies, leeks, celery, shallots, and carrots. Sauté in the lobster butter until the vegetables are softened.

4. Add the white wine, the herbs, and the cooking liquid or the combination of water and chicken stock to cover, and simmer on low heat for 45 minutes.

5. Strain the Lobster Stock, discarding the vegetables and shells. Return the stock to the pot and whisk in the tomato paste. Bring to a boil and reduce to about 3 cups.

MAKES 3 CUPS

LOBSTER TERMS

Bugs: Slang term for lobsters, often used by fishermen

Chicken lobsters or chix: Lobsters weighing between 1 and 1¼ pounds

Cull: A lobster with only one claw

Hard shell: Lobsters before the molt whose shells have hardened up. These have less liquid and more meat.

Jumbos: Lobsters weighing more than 2½ pounds

Pound and a quarters: Self explanatory

Selects: Lobsters from 1½ to 2½ pounds

Shedders: Soft shell lobsters that have just molted. These have more liquid and proportionately less meat, though the meat is often very tender.

Tomalley: The lobster's liver, considered by many to be a great delicacy

NEW ENGLAND LOBSTER CASSEROLE

This recipe is adapted from a Maine Lobster Promotion Council recipe found on its Web site (www.mainelobsterpromo.com). The council offers lots of information on lobsters, lobstering, and classic recipes as well as newer ones. In the late 1800s when the lobster canning industry was in full swing, every frugal New England housewife had a recipe for Lobster Casserole. At that time a can of lobster cost about five cents. Although canned lobster isn't available anymore, at least to my knowledge, this savory casserole is a wonderful—if less frugal—way to enjoy lobster, especially in the cooler months.

8 tablespoons butter, divided

1 pound cooked lobster meat, cut into bite-size pieces

1/3 cup flour

3/4 teaspoon dry mustard

1 cup milk

1 cup Lobster Stock (see the recipe in this chapter) or seafood stock

Sea salt and fresh-ground pepper, to taste

8 ounces sliced mushrooms

1 garlic clove, finely chopped

1 tablespoon chopped fresh parsley

1 cup crumbled Pilot crackers or oyster crackers

Tomato and cucumber slices, for serving

1. Preheat the oven to 350°F.

2. In a saucepan, melt 3 tablespoons of the butter. Briefly sauté the lobster meat in the butter until it starts to turn pink. With a slotted spoon, remove the meat. Add 2 more tablespoons of butter and melt. Whisk the flour and dry mustard into the butter.

3. Stir in the milk and Lobster Stock, bring to a simmer, and cook until thickened, whisking constantly. Season to taste with sea salt and fresh pepper.

4. In a sauté pan, melt the remaining 3 tablespoons butter. Sauté the mushrooms until they just start to give up their water. Remove the mushrooms from the pan. Stir the cooked lobster meat and sautéed mushrooms into the lobster sauce.

5. Add the garlic, parsley, and crackers to the mushroom butter. Stir well to combine.

6. Grease a large casserole dish. Spoon the lobster-mushroom mixture into the bottom of the casserole. Cover with the buttered crackers.

7. Bake until bubbly and the top is golden brown, about 20 to 30 minutes. Serve with tomato and cucumber slices.

SERVES 4

LOBSTER CROQUETTES

This recipe is adapted from *The Rumford Complete Cookbook* by Lily Haxworth Wallace, a "lecturer, teacher and writer on domestic science." The book was first published by the Rumford Company in Providence, Rhode Island, in 1908. These would make an excellent hors d'oeuvre or brunch dish with eggs. Handle the croquettes gently as they are rather delicate.

½ pound cooked lobster meat

2 teaspoons butter

3 teaspoons flour

½ cup warm milk

Salt and pepper, to taste

1 teaspoon lemon juice

Pinch of nutmeg

1 egg, lightly beaten

2 tablespoons dry bread crumbs

Vegetable oil, for frying

Cocktail or tartar sauce, for
   serving

1. Finely chop the lobster meat, adding the "coral" or red roe if there is any.

2. Melt the butter and stir in the flour until well blended. Add the warm milk and whisk to a thick white sauce. Add the salt, pepper, lemon juice, and nutmeg, and mix well.

3. While the mixture is still hot, add the lobster and let it cool. When it's cool, lightly flour and shape into patties or small rolls.

4. Dip each croquette into the beaten egg, then into the bread crumbs, and fry in ¼ inch oil until golden brown. Serve with cocktail or tartar sauce.

SERVES 4

LOBSTER BYTE

A lobster is approximately seven years old before it is legal to harvest, and it will weigh about one pound.

—Courtesy of the Maine Lobster Promotion Council

GRILLED LOBSTER WITH AVOCADO-LIME MAYONNAISE

Many lobster purists resist the idea of grilling lobster, convinced that it is best boiled or steamed, period. While I am a devoted consumer of simple boiled lobster, this is a fun summer dish for a cookout.

FOR THE AVOCADO-LIME MAYONNAISE

2 ripe avocados, peeled and diced

¾ cup mayonnaise

Juice of 1 lime, or more to taste

1 teaspoon grated lime zest

Dash of hot sauce

Salt and pepper, to taste

FOR THE LOBSTER

3 lobsters, 1½–2 pounds each

Olive oil

Sea salt and white pepper, to taste

Lime wedges, for serving

1. Make the Mayonnaise: Blend the first five ingredients until smooth. Add salt and pepper to taste and refrigerate until ready to serve.

2. Prepare the Lobster: Preheat a gas or charcoal grill to medium.

3. Parboil the lobsters for 5 to 6 minutes, and let them cool just enough that you can handle them.

4. Twist off the claws with knuckles attached. Break off tail and split lengthwise with a sharp knife. Remove the intestines in the tail and rinse off any other debris. (A professional chef might well insist on splitting a lobster in half lengthwise while it is still alive, but for the more fainthearted among us, I suggest parboiling.) Discard the bodies or reserve for stock.

5. Brush the lobsters with olive oil and season lightly with sea salt and white pepper.

6. Place the lobster tails shell-side down and cook for 5 minutes over medium heat, brushing with more oil several times. Put the whole claws on the grill to finish cooking. Turn the lobster tails over for 5 minutes or so, enough to sear the meat.

7. Serve with Avocado-Lime Mayonnaise and garnish with lime wedges.

SERVES 6

Note: This recipe is best with hard-shell lobsters. Soft-shell lobsters have more liquid and the result is more of a poached effect.

LOBSTER AND ASPARAGUS RISOTTO WITH TRUFFLE OIL

This is a luxurious combination that is best when both lobster and fresh asparagus are in season. It's an excellent first course or lunch dish. The truffle oil adds the final sumptuous touch.

4 lobsters, 1–1¼ pounds each, or
  1 pound lobster meat
1½ pounds asparagus
2 cups vegetable stock or
  Lobster Stock (see the recipe
  in this chapter)
1½ cups white wine
2 cups water, more as needed
1 tablespoon butter
2 tablespoons oil
2 shallots, minced
1 clove garlic, minced
2 cups Arborio rice
Salt and pepper, to taste
Truffle oil, to taste

1. Boil the lobsters for 10 minutes or until cooked. Remove the meat, and slice the tail and knuckle meat into ½-inch pieces. Try to keep the claws whole. You can also buy ready-cooked lobster meat by the pound.

2. Break off the tough ends of the asparagus and steam for 3 to 5 minutes, depending on the size of the stalks. They should be just cooked through and still a bit crunchy. Cut into 1-inch pieces, reserving the tips.

3. Bring the stock, wine, and water just to a simmer. Keep this on the stove where you will be cooking the risotto.

4. Heat the butter and oil in a wide, heavy pot. Sauté the shallots and garlic until soft and translucent.

5. Add the Arborio rice and stir for 1 to 2 minutes, until well coated.

6. Begin adding the simmering stock ½ cup at a time. Stir the risotto each time after adding the broth until the liquid is absorbed. Cook the rice until tender but still firm, approximately 20 minutes.

7. A minute or two before the risotto is finished cooking, stir in the lobster tail and knuckle meat and pieces of asparagus stalks. Toss lightly. Season to taste with salt and pepper.

8. Top each portion with a claw or piece of claw and asparagus tips. Drizzle each portion lightly with truffle oil and serve.

SERVES 6

BUTTER-POACHED LOBSTER MEDALLIONS WITH PISTACHIO AND WHITE TRUFFLE OIL

Derek Sarno, a veteran chef, restaurateur, and owner of Mizuna Cafe in Portsmouth, New Hampshire, lived on Little Cranberry Island near Mount Desert Island in Maine for several years before coming to Portsmouth. He was a stern man—that is, a captain's assistant—on a lobster boat and ran a restaurant in the summer. He says, "I found that lobster is best to have just plain, though there is nothing plain about this recipe. It's great as a hors d'oeuvre or casual snack—an expensive snack, though." He goes on, "I prefer northern Maine lobster; they tend to be sweeter with the colder water."

8 sticks (2 pounds) unsalted butter

3 cups water

1 lobster, about 1¼ pounds

½ cup shelled pistachios

White truffle oil, to taste

1. Melt the butter in a pot with the water. Bring to a simmer.
2. Add the lobster. The key is not to boil the lobster but to slowly poach it with the butter for the flavor to penetrate. Simmer for 12 minutes or until the lobster is bright red.
3. When the lobster is done, remove it from the liquid, let it cool, and pick the meat out of the shell.
4. Clean and slice the tail into medallions.
5. Crush the pistachios in a food processor, or crush them into a fine dust with a mallet or the bottom of a heavy pan.
6. Sprinkle pistachio dust onto the lobster pieces, and drizzle with white truffle oil before serving.

SERVES 4-6 AS AN APPETIZER

LOBSTER BYTE

A lobster will commonly store food by burying it on the bottom of the ocean and defending the area much like a dog.

—Courtesy of the Maine Lobster Promotion Council

"Baltimore lay very near the protein factory of Chesapeake Bay
and out of the bay it ate divinely . . .
prime hard crabs of the channel species, blue in color,
at least eight inches in length along the shell,
and with snow white meat almost as firm as soap."

—H. L. MENCKEN

Crab

There are many species of crab worldwide. In northern New England the most common are rock and Jonah crabs, which are surprisingly meaty. But the variety that constitutes most of the American crab fishery is the Atlantic blue crab, found roughly from Cape Cod, Massachusetts, on down the eastern seaboard. The other important species from a culinary point of view is Florida's stone crabs, whose claws are particularly prized, the Pacific Dungeness crabs, and of course Alaskan king crab. All are delicious, and the meat can be used interchangeably with the crabmeat specified in this chapter's recipes, though many would say that some of these delicacies are best enjoyed "neat" with perhaps some drawn butter.

About 50 percent of the eastern crab catch comes from the Chesapeake Bay, and that part of the country is justifiably famous for its crab cuisine. I have fond memories of a noisy, messy, and thoroughly enjoyable crab dinner in Maryland. The typical crab shack experience involves tables covered with newspaper, mallets for cracking the crab, spicy crab boil seasoning, and pitchers of ice-cold beer. It's not pretty, but boy, is it good.

"Picking" a crab is even more challenging than eating a lobster. The shells can be as hard or harder, and there is a smaller quantity of meat. Crab shacks often bring them a dozen to the order. Most of the meat is contained in the claws, though it's worth picking through to get the "lump" crabmeat from the body, as well as the "backfin" meat. Veteran crab pickers can pry and crack their way to about 2¼ ounces of meat per crab.

Although not as plentiful a fishery as it was twenty years ago, crabs are caught off the New England coast by lobstermen as a secondary catch. Often, for those anglers who had a patient wife at home willing to pick and pack the meat, it was supplemental income. More and more, our canned crab—like so many other products—is coming from Southeast Asia, where there are plentiful supplies of crab as well as cheap labor.

The only time when crabs are not so labor intensive is when they have molted and shed their hard shell. Before the new shell hardens again, they are sold and served as soft-shell crab. The first time you try one, it may seem odd to eat the crab claws, legs, and all, but they have incredible flavor and can be prepared quite simply. Blue crabs are the only crabs available in this form.

Live blue crabs in the pot ready for cooking.

CRAB LANGUAGE

According to the Blue Crab Archives (blue-crab.org), male hard-shell crabs, preferred for their larger size and greater quantity of meat, are known as "jimmies." Adult female crabs are known as "sooks." They are graded numerically, with number one jimmies being the largest and meatiest crab available. Number twos are usually smaller male crabs, and number threes are a mixture of ungraded smaller crabs, which may contain both male and female. "Busters" are crabs that are just about to shed their shell, while "peelers" are those that have just shed.

The Blue Crab Home Page (www.blue-crab.net) tells us: "The scientific name (*Callinectes sapidus* Rathbun) of the blue crab aptly describes the species. It was derived from Latin and Greek: *Calli*, beautiful; *nectes*, swimmer; and, *sapidus*, savory. A literal translation might be the beautiful, savory swimmer. Rathbun refers to the late Dr. Mary Rathbun, who described the species in 1896."

BASIC BOILED OR STEAMED BLUE CRABS

A visit with friends and family in Maryland often includes a wonderfully messy, noisy, and tasty crab feast. Traditionally a big table is covered with old newspaper and the crabs are cracked with big mallets and picked apart with your fingers. As my brother, who lives in Maryland, writes: "The number of crabs per serving varies greatly, depends on the size of the crabs and one's inclination. Nowadays, I'll typically eat four large crabs, but I certainly remember eating a dozen or more mediums, back in the day. They have gotten a good deal more expensive, and I don't want as much to eat. I suspect four is a decent planning number, maybe more if the crabs are mediums. Most people weary of the labor before their desire for more crab wanes. Like lobster, and unlike a Big Mac, part of the allure of cracking crabs is that you never really have enough to be fully satisfied. Each crab is always an appetizer for the next."

¼ cup vinegar

¼ cup seasoning, such as
   Old Bay

1 teaspoon salt

2 dozen lively blue crabs

1. Fill a large pot or Dutch oven with an inch or two of water. Add the vinegar, Old Bay or other seasoning, and salt.

2. Place a steaming rack in the bottom of the pot and bring the water to a boil.

3. Add the crabs, layering them in the pot, and steam for 30 minutes. Serve with lots of napkins and plenty of cold beer.

SERVES 4-6

BAY SEASONING

Hard crabs are sold by the dozen or bushel, with a bushel of number ones containing sixty to seventy crabs. If you are planning a crab boil, allow about six crabs per person. As with lobsters, look for lively ones and use them as close to the time of purchase as possible. Discard any that seem limp or lifeless.

The Blue Crab Archives (blue-crab.org) offers this spice mixture recipe that you can make yourself.

1 tablespoon sea salt

1 tablespoon celery salt

1 tablespoon ground dry mustard

1 tablespoon paprika

½ tablespoon mace

½ teaspoon cinnamon

½ teaspoon red pepper

½ teaspoon black pepper

½ teaspoon crushed red pepper
   flakes

¼ teaspoon ground cloves

1. Mix all the spices together and store in an airtight container.
2. Add ½ cup or so when boiling or steaming crabs.

A sailor holding two red crabs aboard the *Albatross III* in 1959.

CRAB AND ARTICHOKE DIP

This simple, savory combination makes a great appetizer or party nibble. It's very quick to prepare, and if you keep canned crabmeat in the pantry, it can easily be thrown together when unexpected guests appear.

1 cup crabmeat

1 14 $\frac{1}{2}$-ounce can artichoke
   hearts, quartered

1$\frac{1}{2}$ cup mayonnaise

1 cup grated Parmesan cheese

3 cloves garlic, crushed

2 shallots, chopped

$\frac{1}{2}$–1 teaspoon hot sauce, to taste

1 tablespoon capers

Salt and pepper, to taste

Crackers or toasted pita chips,
   for serving

1. In a food processor, blend all the ingredients until well blended but not smooth.

2. Place the mixture in a ramekin or small casserole dish. Heat until bubbling and heated through. Serve with crackers or toasted pita chips.

SERVES 6–8 AS AN HORS D'OEUVRE

CRAB LOUIS

This is a classic but simple dish that makes a great appetizer or light lunch. Use the best crabmeat you can find. It's very similar to a Creole crab remoulade.

1½ pounds lump crabmeat

1 cup mayonnaise

¼ cup heavy cream

¼ cup chili sauce

2 tablespoons chopped scallions

2 tablespoons finely chopped
   green pepper

1 tablespoon chopped pitted
   green olives

1 tablespoon fresh lemon juice

1. Divide the crabmeat among six chilled plates.

2. In a small bowl, combine the remaining ingredients and mix well.

3. Place a dollop of sauce on each plate and serve.

SERVES 6

Sorting crabs.

CRAB CAKES

There are probably as many recipes for crab cakes as there are cooks in the Chesapeake Bay area. Most people agree that more crab and less filler is the way to go.

¼ cup minced shallots

¼ cup minced green bell
   peppers

½ tablespoon olive oil

1 pound lump crabmeat, drained

12 saltine crackers, crushed

2 egg whites, lightly beaten

2 tablespoons mayonnaise

1 tablespoon fresh lemon juice

½ teaspoon Dijon mustard

Sea salt and white pepper,
   to taste

Dash of hot sauce

1½ tablespoons vegetable oil

Lemons, for serving

Tartar or cocktail sauce, for
   serving

1. In a small skillet, sauté the shallots and peppers in the olive oil until soft.

2. In a large bowl, combine all the remaining ingredients except the vegetable oil. Mix lightly with your hands until well combined. Divide into eight cakes.

3. Chill the cakes in the refrigerator for at least half an hour before cooking.

4. Heat the vegetable oil in a large skillet over high heat. Add the crab cakes and cook until golden brown on each side, about 4 minutes per side. Serve immediately with lemons and tartar sauce or cocktail sauce.

MAKES 8 CAKES

CRAB CIOPPINO

People have strong opinions about seafood stews such as cioppino and bouillabaisse, insisting that only a certain array of ingredients make them "authentic." My feeling is that most of these dishes originated with fishermen who were throwing into their soup pots whatever was left from their catch. We should feel free to do the same. Experiment with your favorite fish and shellfish.

If you can make this early in the day or even the night before, the flavors will have time to blend, develop, and grow even more delicious.

¼ cup olive oil

1 large onion, peeled

1 tablespoon minced garlic

1 stalk celery, chopped fine

1 green pepper, coarsely chopped

¼ cup chopped Italian flat-leaf
   parsley

¼ cup chopped fresh oregano

1 28-ounce can whole Italian
   plum tomatoes

1 6-ounce can tomato paste

1 cup clam juice

1 cup water

2 cups dry red wine

18 littleneck clams

12 large shrimp, unpeeled

1 pound lump crabmeat

Crusty bread, for serving

1. In a large pot or Dutch oven, heat the olive oil over medium heat. Add the onion, garlic, celery, and pepper, and sauté until soft. Add the parsley and oregano.

2. Add the tomatoes, tomato paste, clam juice, water, and wine to the vegetables and slowly bring to a boil. Simmer over low heat for 10 minutes.

3. Add the clams and simmer for 3 minutes. Then add the shrimp and crab and simmer for another 3 minutes, or until the shrimp are pink, the clams are open, and everything is heated through. Serve with warm, crusty bread.

SERVES 4-6

INDIVIDUAL MAINE CRABMEAT SOUFFLÉS

This mouthwatering brunch dish is inspired by the beautiful 1794 Watchtide by the Sea Inn, on the waterfront in Searsport, Maine. This lovely home was first owned by Brig. Gen. Henry Knox, one of George Washington's most valuable senior officers who later became the new nation's first secretary of war. The inn is known for its outstanding breakfasts.

2 tablespoons melted butter

1 pound Maine crabmeat

3 eggs

½ cup heavy cream

1 cup Gruyère or Emmenthaler
   cheese

½ cup grated Parmesan cheese

Pinch of nutmeg

Pinch of thyme

Few grains of cayenne or hot
   sauce

Salt and pepper, to taste

1. Preheat the oven to 450°F.

2. Brush the insides of six ramekins with the melted butter. Divide the crabmeat among the ramekins, covering the bottom of each with crabmeat.

3. Separate the eggs and whisk the yolks together with the cream until light. Add any remaining butter and mix in the cheeses. Add the nutmeg, thyme, and cayenne, and season to taste with salt and pepper.

4. Whisk the egg whites to form stiff peaks; gently fold into yolk-cheese mixture. Gently spoon the soufflé mixture into the ramekins, filling each two-thirds full. Place the ramekins in a baking dish and add warm water to come halfway up their sides. Bake for 15 minutes, till the soufflés rise and their tops are puffed and golden brown. Serve immediately.

SERVES 6

PAN-FRIED SOFT-SHELL CRAB

Soft-shell crabs are just hard-shell crabs that have shed their shell and the new one has yet to harden. It's a strange thing to eat the whole crab—I must admit I was skeptical the first time I tried it—but they are incredibly delicious and can be quite simple to prepare. Ask your fishmonger to "dress" them for you if possible. Otherwise a quick Internet search for "blue crabs" will yield a host of sites with instructions, recipes, and background.

1 cup flour

1 teaspoon sea salt

1 teaspoon Old Bay Seasoning

12 soft-shell crabs, cleaned and
    dressed

1 cup vegetable oil, or enough to
    cover the bottom of a large
    skillet about ½ inch deep

2 tablespoons butter

Lemon wedges, for serving

1. Mix together the flour, salt, and seafood seasoning.

2. Dredge the crabs in the flour mixture to coat well.

3. In a large frying pan or electric skillet, heat about ½ inch cooking oil to 375°F. Add butter.

4. Add the crabs and reduce the heat to 350°F. Cook the crabs until browned, about 5 minutes on each side. Serve hot with lemon wedges.

SERVES 6 (2 CRABS EACH)

"I be pickerin' it in my head,
standin' at the wheel of the shrimp boat—or even better,
settin' there on the back of the boat, eatin' shrimp!"

—FORREST GUMP

Shrimp

Shrimp are incredibly versatile. They are also one of the most globally appreciated seafoods, with major fisheries in the United States, Southeast Asia, and South America, and welcoming consumers worldwide. They are an important part of many cuisines, from Japanese to Creole. Still, the United States is the largest market—in 2003 we imported more than 500,000 tons *beyond* the shrimp caught and farmed in our home waters. Fortunately, shrimp aquaculture has been highly successful, since our hunger for them seems to grow every year.

The shrimp we enjoy in restaurants, frozen, or fresh from our supermarket, if caught in American waters at all, most likely came from the southern Atlantic or Gulf of Mexico. There are numerous species with a variety of names, but the vast majority of what we consume are either Pacific white shrimp or giant tiger prawns. In general the words *shrimp* and *prawn* are used interchangeably, although some people refer to larger shrimp as prawns.

The tiny northern shrimp is the variety caught off the New England coast and is available for only a few months during winter. Sadly, when poor catches kept native New England shrimp out of the markets for several years running, consumers became accustomed to their absence. Although the shrimp catch has improved, the demand for them hasn't fully recovered. That's a shame, because native New England shrimp are one of the great delicacies of our cold northern waters.

Although people have been catching northern shrimp since the 1600s, there was no commercial fishery until sometime in the twentieth century. These small specimens were used primarily for bait. It wasn't until canned shrimp from the South became available that shrimp began to be a popular ingredient. Cookbooks from the early 1900s reveal little interest in shrimp. Amazing, considering the amount we now consume. And why not? Shrimp are low cal, low fat, fast and easy to prepare, not to mention delicious.

HOW TO PEEL AND DEVEIN SHRIMP

To shell a shrimp, hold the tail in one hand while gently removing the shell around the body with the other. You can get rid of the tail shell altogether, or leave it on for appearance and as a handy handle for dipping into cocktail sauce. To remove the vein (as in "devein the shrimp," although it is actually an intestine), make a shallow cut lengthwise down the outer curve of the shrimp's tail. Pick out the dark vein that runs lengthwise down the shrimp's back by using a pointy utensil or scraping the vein off with your fingertip while rinsing under running water.

CHILLED NORTHERN SHRIMP SALAD IN AVOCADO

This makes a lovely light lunch or first course. A sliced tomato would be a nice accompaniment.

3 ripe avocados

2 teaspoons lemon juice

1½ cups small cooked shrimp (or substitute crab or lobster)

½ cup mayonnaise

½ teaspoon grated lemon rind

Salt and pepper, to taste

½ teaspoon paprika

1. Split the avocados lengthwise and remove their pits. Brush with lemon juice to prevent them from browning.

2. In a small bowl, combine the remaining ingredients except the paprika. Fill each avocado half with the shrimp mixture. Sprinkle with paprika. Cover and chill until ready to serve.

SERVES 6 AS AN APPETIZER

A full and successful catch of fresh shrimp in the hold of a boat, together with a bucket used to bring the shrimp to the sorting table.

MAINE SHRIMP RISOTTO WITH PROSCIUTTO AND PEAS

This wonderful dish comes from chef-owner Rob Evans of Hugo's Restaurant in Portland, Maine. Evans was named one of *Food and Wine*'s Top 10 Hottest New Chefs in 2005. This recipe calls for carnaroli rice, which is a lovely, flavor-absorbing, translucent rice from Italy. If you can't find this, feel free to use Arborio rice, which may be easier to find. If you can't find northern shrimp, use small frozen shrimp.

2 tablespoon canola oil

1 small onion, diced

6 cloves of garlic, minced

¼ teaspoon crushed red pepper

1 teaspoon ground coriander

1 teaspoon ground cumin

1 teaspoon paprika

1 cup carnaroli or Arborio rice

½ cup white wine

2 quarts shrimp or seafood
  stock, hot

1 pound cleaned Maine shrimp,
  plus more for garnish

2 tablespoons cold butter

1 tablespoon Mascarpone cheese

1 cup fresh or frozen peas

½ teaspoon lemon juice

1 cup fresh grated Parmesan
  cheese

1 tablespoon thyme, chopped

Salt and pepper, to taste

8 thin slices of prosciutto

1. Heat the oil in a large heavy-bottomed pan. Add the onion, garlic, red pepper, coriander, cumin, and paprika and cook over low heat until vegetables are soft.

2. Add rice and gently stir for 3 minutes to coat the rice. Add wine and continue cooking until rice has absorbed all the liquid.

3. Add a third of the stock and stir continually to be sure the rice is not browning on the bottom. When stock is mostly absorbed, ladle more stock into the rice. Continue adding liquid and stirring until rice is al dente or just firm in the middle of the grains.

4. Stir in shrimp, butter, Mascarpone, peas, lemon juice, grated Parmesan, and thyme and season to taste with salt and pepper. Adjust consistency so risotto runs level in the pan.

5. Line four bowls with two slices each of the prosciutto and fold over ends. Garnish with whole peeled shrimp if desired.

SERVES 4

POTTED SHRIMP

This is an updated New England adaptation of a popular British dish of the 1800s that was served as either an appetizer or a "savoury," which came after the main dish. Northern shrimp lend themselves well to this because they are so tender.

4 tablespoons softened butter, divided

3 shallots, finely chopped

½ pound northern shrimp, peeled

Salt and pepper, to taste

2 tablespoons white vermouth

½ cup cream cheese, softened

1 tablespoon fresh lemon juice

1 tablespoon chopped fresh dill

1 teaspoon Worcestershire sauce

Pinch of mace

Hot sauce, to taste

Water crackers, for serving

1. In a medium skillet, melt 1 tablespoon of the butter over moderate heat. Sauté the shallots until soft. Add the shrimp, along with salt and pepper to taste, and cook, stirring occasionally, until the shrimp are pink and just cooked through, about 1 to 2 minutes.

2. Add the vermouth and bring to a boil. Remove the mixture from the heat and transfer the shrimp to a cutting board. When they're cool, chop the shrimp coarsely.

3. In a food processor, blend the remaining butter and cream cheese. Add the shrimp, shallots, lemon juice, dill, Worcestershire sauce, mace, and pan juices and pulse just long enough to blend.

4. Season to taste with more salt and pepper, and with hot sauce. Chill for at least 4 hours. Serve with water crackers.

SERVES 4–6 AS AN HORS D'OEUVRE

SHRIMP AND CLAMS CATAPLANA

Found in the coastal regions of Portugal, cataplana dishes use a copper cookpot with a hinged lid to cook shellfish with ham or sausage. By the late 1800s there was a large Portuguese population in New England, many of whom had come to work in the thriving fisheries out of Gloucester, Fall River, and New Bedford, Massachusetts. There are still thriving Portuguese communities in these towns. This dish is inspired by and a tribute to their culinary traditions.

4 tablespoons olive oil, divided

1½ cups chorizo, cut in half
   lengthwise and then sliced

3 tablespoons chopped garlic

¾ cup shallots, thinly sliced

1 cup sliced leeks

¾ cup white wine

¾ cup clam juice or fish stock

2 dozen littleneck clams

1 pound shell-on medium shrimp

Crusty bread, for serving

1. In a large pot with a tight-fitting lid or a cataplana, heat 2 tablespoons of the olive oil. Add the chorizo and lightly brown for about 5 minutes. Remove the chorizo and reserve.

2. Add the garlic, shallots, and leeks, and sauté until soft and golden. Add the wine and clam juice or fish stock; bring to a simmer. Add the clams, cover, and cook for 5 minutes. Add the shrimp, cover, and cook for another 3 minutes or until the shrimp are pink and cooked through.

3. Spoon portions of clams, shrimp, and chorizo into bowls. Drizzle the remaining olive oil atop and serve with plenty of crusty bread.

SERVES 4

CAJUN SHRIMP SAUTÉ

Most of the recipes in this chapter can be made with either northern shrimp or larger Gulf shrimp. For this particular recipe, I prefer the larger Gulf shrimp, as they are better suited to stronger, spicier flavors. This makes a great appetizer or entree served over rice. Don't be daunted by the long list of ingredients—the dish is actually quite simple.

1 tablespoon chile powder

1 tablespoon dark brown sugar, firmly packed

1 teaspoon celery salt

1 teaspoon cumin

½ teaspoon white pepper

½ teaspoon dried thyme

1 teaspoon garlic powder

1 pound medium shrimp, peeled

2 tablespoons olive oil

¼ cup chopped cubanelle or poblano peppers (or substitute jalapeños or Anaheims for more heat)

⅓ cup chopped yellow onion

⅓ cup chopped scallions

¼ cup white wine

Lemon wedges, for serving

1. In a small bowl, mix together the dry ingredients. Toss the shrimp in this mixture to coat.

2. In a large skillet, heat the olive oil, add the peppers, onion, and scallions, and sauté until soft. Add the shrimp and wine, and cook over medium heat until the shrimp are pink and firm, about 3 to 4 minutes. Serve hot with lemon wedges.

SERVES 2-4

Southern shrimp boats drying their nets, circa 1960.

MAINE SHRIMP BISQUE

You could use just about any smaller shrimp, but in New England, when northern shrimp are in season—from about December to March—it's fairly easy to find shrimp with the heads on. This isn't essential, but the heads add extra flavor to the stock.

   Although this dish is somewhat labor intensive, the final product is a delicate bisque that will reward your efforts. It makes a lovely cold-weather lunch or supper with a green salad and crusty bread.

2 pounds northern shrimp, heads and shells on

1 cup white wine or dry vermouth

2 cups water, divided

1 bay leaf

3 tablespoons butter, divided

1 tablespoon olive oil

⅓ cup chopped celery

⅓ cup chopped shallots

⅓ cup chopped carrots

2 tablespoons flour

2 tablespoons tomato paste

1 teaspoon sea salt

½ teaspoon white pepper

½ teaspoon Old Bay Seasoning

¼ teaspoon dry mustard

1 pint (2 cups) light cream

2 tablespoons sherry

1. Remove the heads from the shrimp; reserve the heads.

2. Combine the wine or vermouth and 1 cup of the water in a large pot. Add the bay leaf and bring to a boil. Add the shrimp tails. Reduce the heat and simmer for 2 minutes. Remove the shrimp from the liquid and plunge into cold water to cool. When they're cool, remove the shells.

3. In the same pot, melt 1 tablespoon of the butter. Add the olive oil, heat through, then add the celery, shallots, and carrots. Sauté until soft, about 7 minutes,

4. Return the shells, the reserved shrimp heads, and the liquid to the pot and simmer over low heat for 20 minutes to make a stock.

5. Strain the liquid though a colander, pressing on the solids.

6. In a saucepan, melt remaining 2 tablespoons of butter. Whisk in the flour to make a roux. Cook over very low heat for 4 to 5 minutes, being careful not to burn the roux.

7. Whisk in the shrimp stock and simmer over low heat for about 5 minutes, until thick and smooth. Add the tomato paste, salt, pepper, Old Bay Seasoning, and dry mustard.

8. Whisk in the cream and sherry and heat through, about a minute. Do not let the soup boil. Serve immediately.

SERVES 6–8

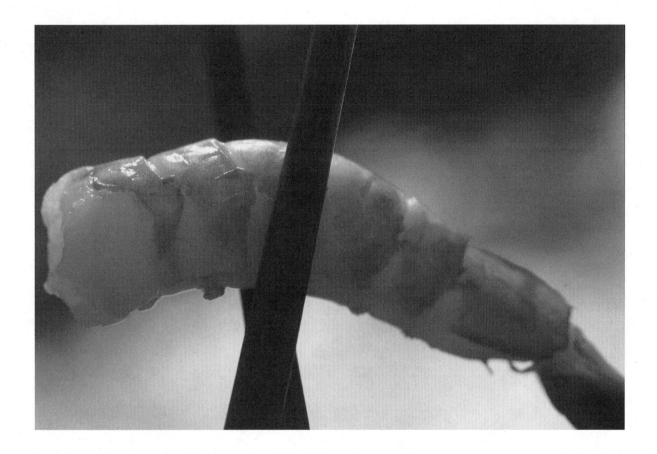

WILD MUSHROOM AND SHRIMP LINGUINI

This is a very quick dish that can be made with any small shrimp. Adjust the garlic up or down to your taste. Serve with crusty bread and a salad for a quick and healthy dinner.

1 pound linguini

¼ cup olive oil

2 leeks, halved, rinsed, and sliced thinly

½ pound mixed "wild" mushrooms, such as oyster, cremini, or shiitake, cleaned and sliced

1 pound small shrimp, shelled

4 cloves garlic, minced

½ cup white vermouth

Salt and fresh pepper, to taste

1 tablespoon thin-sliced basil

⅔ cup grated Parmesan cheese

1. Bring a large pot of salted water to a boil. Add the pasta and cook according to the package directions.

2. While the linguini is cooking, heat the olive oil in a large pot or deep skillet. Add the leeks and sauté over low heat until soft and golden. Add the mushrooms and sauté until soft and shiny.

3. Add the shrimp, garlic, and white vermouth and cook until just cooked through, about 2 minutes.

4. Drain the pasta, reserving ½ cup of the pasta liquid. Add the linguini to the shrimp-mushroom mixture. Stir well, adding enough of the pasta water to create a thin sauce. Season with salt and pepper. Top with basil and cheese and serve immediately.

SERVES 4–6

BARBECUED SHRIMP SKEWERS

This recipe is best done with large shrimp. They hold up to grilling or broiling better, and their slightly stronger flavor pairs well with flavorful marinades like this one.

½ cup olive oil

⅓ cup soy sauce

2 tablespoons rice wine vinegar

1 tablespoon brown sugar

1 tablespoon minced garlic

1 teaspoon Asian sesame oil

1 teaspoon grated orange rind

1 pound large shrimp, shells split
  lengthwise but left on

Lemon wedges, for serving

1. Combine all the ingredients except the shrimp and lemon wedges in a small bowl. Whisk until well combined.

2. In a glass dish or resealable plastic bag, marinate the shrimp in this mixture for at least 30 minutes and up to 2 hours.

3. Thread the shrimp onto metal or bamboo skewers that have been soaked in water to prevent scorching.

4. Grill over medium heat for about 2 minutes per side or until the shrimp are firm and pink. Serve warm or at room temperature with lemon wedges.

SERVES 4–6 AS AN HORS D'OEUVRE

PART THREE
FIN FISH

"It's no fish yer buying, it's men's lives."

—SIR WALTER SCOTT

Fish of the North Atlantic

This section of *Mystic Seafood* is devoted to "swimming" fish, or more accurately fin fish (since some shellfish can swim). I've focused primarily on fish that are relatively common in the Northeast, since so much of the history of our country—and the history documented at Mystic Seaport—took place here.

In many ways the history of the New England fisheries is the history of New England. The first settlers may have come to escape religious oppression, but the subsequent story of survival—and success—is one very big fish story.

When the first settlers arrived, they found a Native population that embraced fish and shellfish as a wonderful and plentiful source of food. The bounty of the sea was fresh, nutritious, and relatively easy to harvest. Fish and shellfish were often the centerpiece of New England tribal gatherings and celebrations. But for the Europeans fish came with the historical baggage of being associated with fast days, Lenten deprivation, and a rather meager substitute for "real" food like beef and pork. (We now know that not only is fish one of the best sources of protein available to us, but it's also low in calories, low in fat, and offers other health benefits.) The fact that seafood was enjoyed so richly by the Native American tribes only strengthened the settlers' prejudices, because it became known as Indian food. It was not until the 1800s that the non-Native population would begin to view seafood as the incredible gift it is.

When Captain John Smith and others first explored New England waters, they didn't find gold or spices, but they did find an abundance of fish—a commodity that would make many fortunes in the centuries to come. Reporting back to England, these intrepid captains described the teeming waters they sailed, and the possibilities were not lost on English investors. Soon transatlantic fishing trips were a common occurrence, and in time New England replaced Newfoundland as the preferred fishing ground.

Since cod could be salted and dried, it became a long-lived staple, and much of the British catch was sold to Portugal and Spain, where the demand for "bacchalao" was perpetual. In the 1700s the sugarcane industry was built on the backs of slaves fed on salt cod. Dried fish of inferior quality was sold to sugarcane plantations in the Caribbean and fed to slaves.

Felix Hogan at the helm of the *L. A. Dunton* on a fishing trip in the 1920s.

By the nineteenth century fishing dominated the economy and the lives of people living around Mystic. The ships still on view at Mystic Seaport provide a wonderful window into the past 200 years of fish and fishing on the East Coast.

Perhaps the most dramatic ship here is the *Charles W. Morgan,* built in 1841 in New Bedford, Massachusetts. For eighty years the Morgan roamed the seas of the world, searching for whales whose blubber the sailors converted to whale oil in the huge trypots on deck.

The *L. A. Dunton* is a Gloucester fisherman of the type used for codfishing on the Grand Banks. Built in 1921, when fishing under sail was beginning to wane in importance, the *Dunton* was used in haddock and halibut fisheries out of Boston, and

The schooner *L. A. Dunton* on the fishing grounds under a shortened rig.

then as a freighter and fishing vessel out of Newfoundland. But it was in the codfishery on the Grand Banks that such Gloucester fishing schooners became most famous. The schooners carried small one- or two-man dories on deck out to the Banks; from there the fishermen handlined for cod until the schooner was full of iced fish. The schooners then raced back to the markets in New England, the first schooners back getting the best price for their fish. They fed the seemingly insatiable demand for cod in the United States and around the Atlantic Ocean from Europe to the Caribbean. Rudyard Kipling's *Captains Courageous* (in both book and movie form) is a vivid depiction of the Grand Banks codfishery.

Not all fish come from the deep ocean, however. *Estella* A. is an example of an inshore fishing boat, in this case a lobster boat; she was built in 1904 and continued lobstering in Maine waters for thirty years. Lobster boats today are driven by powerful engines, but the techniques are basically the same: The traps are baited and left on the ocean bottom, with a buoy and line to haul them back up. The lobsterman on *Estella* A. hauled each trap up by hand, kept the legal-size lobsters, rebaited the trap, and sent it back into the ocean. Most lobstering goes on within sight of land; the boats and their catch return to port every night. Lobstering today is one of the great success stories in American fishing. The lobster population is stable, and the fishery is well regulated to prevent overfishing.

Emma C. Berry—built in 1866 in the Noank River two miles from Mystic—is one of the oldest surviving commercial vessels in America. She was used for general fishing and cargo carrying for nearly sixty years. Unlike the deep-sea vessels that iced or salted their catch, the *Emma C.* was fitted with a live well in her hold where seawater freely circulated, keeping the catch alive until it could be delivered to market.

With the dragger *Roann* we leave behind 300 years of fishing under sail. *Roann* has a diesel engine to pull her dragnets through the water, hauling the catch aboard over the side of the sixty-foot ship. *Roann* fished for cod, haddock, and flounder from the island of Martha's Vineyard and then from Point Judith, Rhode Island. *Roann*'s type was common into the 1970s, when faster and more powerful draggers converted to more efficient stern hauling of their nets.

Today our fishing boats are working harder and harder and we are eating more fish than ever: 16.6 pounds per capita in 2004, up from 11.5 pounds in 1910. The U.S. fishery brings in some 9.6 billion pounds a year. Sound like a lot? Actually the United States ranks fifth in total annual catch, behind China, Peru, India, and Indonesia. Sadly, our supplies are diminishing, and our exports increasing. We can only hope that, with luck and proper management, our fisheries will not go the way of some of the Scandinavian countries, where abundant catches are only a memory and once prosperous fishing villages are nearly abandoned.

Future abundance may well depend on our ability to perfect aquaculture and to broaden our tastes so that underused species can add diversity to our diets. Fish that have been used widely in Europe are now gaining popularity thanks to a generation of inventive new chefs, who have provided us with some wonderfully creative recipes.

Mystic Seaport's eastern rig dragger *Roann* in 1977 at the end of her fishing career.

HOW TO CHOOSE GOOD FISH

When it comes to seafood, the nose always knows. Any fish that smells "fishy" is not something you want to take home. Good fresh fish has very little smell, except for a briny, oceany scent. Any hint of ammonia or off-smell means the fish is past its sell-by date. Most fish are more readily available in steaks or fillets than whole. When choosing these, look for firm, moist pieces. A dry appearance or dull color usually means a second-rate product.

If you have the opportunity to choose a whole fish, look for bright clear eyes and red gills, as opposed to gray or brown, another indicator of age. Most New England fish markets that have been around for any length of time will stock only quality seafoods, but it's always okay to ask what's best on that day or what has come in most recently. It sounds weird, but don't be afraid to ask to smell the fish, too. I have a few local sources that I use, and developing a relationship with your fishmonger is a surefire way to get the freshest and the best.

The dangers of eating certain kinds of fish have been flashed about in the news quite a lot lately, but it would be a shame to avoid fish and all its health benefits because of worries about mercury. The fact is that the primary concerns are for pregnant women, babies, and young children. According to the Environmental Protection Agency (EPA), "Research shows that most people's fish consumption does not cause a health concern. However, high levels of mercury in the bloodstream of unborn babies and young children may harm the developing nervous system. With this in mind, the Food and Drug Administration and EPA designed an advisory that if followed should keep an individual's mercury consumption below levels that have been shown to cause harm. By following the advisory parents can be confident of reducing their unborn or young child's exposure to the harmful effects of mercury, while at the same time maintaining a healthy diet that includes the nutritional benefits of fish and shellfish." If you are concerned, please visit www.epa.gov, and look under "Fish Consumption Advisories" in the "Mercury" section.

Bass

In mid-nineteenth century southern New England, fishing for bass was a favorite summer pastime. Excursion boats took residents of the sweltering cities out for a day of fishing on Long Island Sound or the Atlantic. In New York City these boats came complete with a live band and cotillion parties on the upper deck. Along with fishing for bass (and other fish), the entertainment included a stop at Coney Island for a swim and a clambake.

Today bass fishing is, if anything, even more popular here, not least because the fish are both fine sport and delicious eating. Two particular—and unrelated—species of bass are most commonly targeted: the striped bass and the black sea bass.

STRIPED BASS

Sitting at my desk in Maine on a July morning, I can see the striped bass fishermen in the cove. There is a motorboat with a few friends fishing on light tackle. They nudge the boat as close to the rocks as they dare and cast their lines in long, graceful arcs. Anglers on the rocks are casting with heavier  gear. On the nearby bridges over the Portsmouth Harbor estuaries, there are fishermen oblivious to the passing cars, focused only on hooking a fierce-fighting striper big enough to keep.

In most places July Fourth is celebrated by cookouts and fireworks. Around here it's also fishing for stripers.

The American Angler's Guide of 1849 is unequivocal in its appreciation of the striped bass: "This noble and highly prized fish is peculiar to our own country, and to particular parts of it. As an object of sport, for perfect symmetry and beauty of appearance, and as a dish for the table, it is considered second only to the salmon."

Striped bass are not related to another Atlantic bass—the black sea bass—but are of the same family as mackerel and bluefish. As with these cousins, stripers' flesh is somewhat oily, so they should be put on ice as soon as they're caught; they're best eaten within twenty-four hours. Although anglers love to hook really big fish, the best ones for the table are less than ten pounds.

Striped bass used to be more than plentiful, as the Pilgrims aboard the *Mayflower* enthusiastically attested. Overfishing and pollution put the species at risk, and while there is still a commercial fishery, the catch has been much reduced in recent decades. Aquaculturists, however, have crossed the striped bass and the white bass and are now raising considerable numbers of farmed "striped bass."

BLACK SEA BASS

The black sea bass is a wonderful fish for the table, with mild white flesh. Most of the fish are around a pound and a half—a good size for cooking whole. The black sea bass is not as beautiful as the striped bass (to which it is not related), but its coal-black color is quite striking and remains so if it's cooked with the skin on.

Color is not the only unusual thing about black sea bass. They are protogynous hermaphrodites, which means that initially they are females, but some larger fish (between nine and thirteen inches) reverse sex to become males, the reversal usually taking place after spawning. Stripers are also protogynous hermaphrodites, but their sexual reversal is the opposite of black bass: male to female.

The black sea bass population is considered to be in pretty good shape in New England and the Mid-Atlantic states. South of that, the species is regarded as overfished.

Sea bass (sometimes the *black* is omitted in their name) may not be as fierce as stripers or bluefish, but pound for pound they make fine sport on light tackle.

"It would be better for the health of those who do not labor, if they would use more fish and less flesh for food. But then fish cannot be rendered so palatable, because it does not admit the variety of cooking and flavors that other animal food does."

—*EARLY AMERICAN COOKERY: THE GOOD HOUSEKEEPER*
BY SARAH JOSEPHA HALE (1841)

SEAFOOD FOR THE STARS

Browne Trading Company in Portland, Maine, is one of the most extraordinary purveyors of fish in the country. Calling the company a fish market is like calling the *Queen Mary* a boat. They were able to supply me with a wonderful whole black bass for the recipe on the next page.

Not only is Browne Trading Company the most diversified importer of caviar in the country, but the company's smoke room produces amazing smoked salmon, finnan haddie, and shellfish, including proprietary varieties for chefs like Daniel Boulud and resellers like Dean and Deluca and Williams Sonoma. Browne Trading Company sells an extraordinary array of seafood both retail and wholesale to customers including Emeril, Charlie Trotter, and Wolfgang Puck. Visit the company's web site: www.browne-trading.com.

SALT-CRUSTED BLACK SEA BASS

This recipe is a personal favorite of Joachim Sandbichler, Austrian-born owner of the award-winning Italian seafood grill Pesce Blue in Portsmouth, New Hampshire. It's also a personal favorite of mine, as is his restaurant. He used to spend his summers on the Italian coast, where branzino, or Mediterranean sea bass, was often served this way. Black sea bass makes a great North Atlantic substitute. Joachim serves this with a simple arugula or tomato salad.

1 2-pound black sea bass

½ lemon, sliced into rounds

4 sprigs tarragon or other fresh herbs

Salt and pepper, to taste

2–3 pounds kosher salt

2–3 tablespoons water

2 tablespoons extra-virgin olive oil

1. Preheat the oven to 400°F.

2. Clean the fish and pat it dry. Place the lemon slices and herbs in the cavity of the cleaned fish; salt and pepper to taste.

3. In a bowl, combine the kosher salt and water. You should be able to form balls that stay together briefly before falling apart.

4. Place a 1-inch-thick layer of the salt paste on the bottom of a baking dish slightly larger than the fish.

5. Rub the bass on all sides with the olive oil. Place the fish on top of the salt layer, and put the rest of the salt on top. Pack it around the fish firmly.

6. Place the fish in the oven and roast for about 30 minutes. Remove the fish and allow it to cool slightly. Remove the salt crust and serve hot.

SERVES 2

"No angling can surpass
The taking of the Basse."

—ANONYMOUS

STRIPED BASS WITH JULIENNED VEGETABLES
AND RED PEPPER COULIS

This great recipe comes from chef Leo Bushey at the award-winning Acqua Oyster Bar in Vernon, Connecticut.

FOR THE COULIS

1 8-ounce jar roasted red peppers

1 medium potato, peeled and cut
  into ½-inch dice

1 carrot, peeled and chopped

2 cloves garlic, peeled

1 medium yellow onion, chopped

3 bottles clam juice, 8 ounces
  each

FOR THE FISH AND VEGETABLES

2 carrots, peeled

1 medium summer squash, halved
  lengthwise and seeded

1 medium zucchini, halved
  lengthwise and seeded

2 tablespoons canola oil

1½ pounds skin-on striped bass
  fillets, cut into 4 equal pieces

Salt and pepper, to taste

1 tablespoon butter

1 shallot, finely chopped

1. Make the Coulis: Put all of the coulis ingredients into a stockpot and simmer for about an hour. Remove from the heat and allow to cool slightly.

2. In a blender or food processor, blend the mixture until smooth. Pour the coulis into a smaller saucepan, adjust the seasonings, and keep warm.

3. Make the Fish and Vegetables: Cut the carrot, summer squash, and zucchini into 2-inch lengths and then julienne into thin lengthwise strips.

4. In a skillet, heat the canola oil over medium-high heat until it's hot but not smoking. Season the fillets with salt and pepper and add to the pan.

5. Cook for 2 to 3 minutes on each side, until the skin is crisp and the fish just cooked through.

6. Remove the fillets to a platter and keep them warm. Wipe out the skillet with a paper towel.

7. Add the butter to the pan and melt over medium-high heat. Add the julienned vegetables and shallot. Stir-fry for 1 to 2 minutes or until just crisp-tender.

8. To serve, spread equal portions of the warm coulis on each plate, top with fish, and serve the vegetables on top.

SERVES 4

BAKED STRIPED BASS WITH BACON

This recipe is adapted from www.fishingworks.com—an amazing resource for anglers of all types. In addition to all the other information the site provides, it has an archive of recipes for just about any kind of fish you can think of. I thought this was a particularly interesting way to prepare striped bass.

4 striped bass fillets, 6–8 ounces each

1 quart golden ginger ale

4 pieces thick-sliced bacon

1 cup sliced baby portobello or cremini mushrooms

1 cup red onion cut into 1-inch slices

4 tablespoons butter

¼ teaspoon dried tarragon

Dash of paprika

1. Soak the bass overnight in the ginger ale in the refrigerator. Rinse when you're ready to cook. Preheat the oven to 350°F.

2. In a pan, cook the bacon until crisp. Remove the bacon from the pan and drain on paper towels. Crumble the bacon and set aside. Cook the mushrooms and onion in the bacon fat till tender.

3. Place the fish in a baking dish. Combine the mushrooms, onion, butter, and tarragon. Spread on top of the fish; sprinkle with paprika. Bake for approximately 20 minutes, until the fish flakes easily. Garnish with the crumbled bacon.

SERVES 4

Bass fishing off the rocks

Bluefish

Fishing for "blues" has been a favorite summer pastime in New England since the 1800s. It's still a popular recreational fishery, but there is a significant commercial catch as well. The number of pounds taken each year since the 1990s was 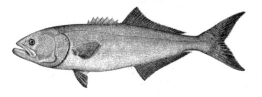 enough to cause the government to issue bluefish restrictions and bag limits, which have been revised periodically. But historically, the number of bluefish has varied widely and cyclically from decade to decade.

As John J. Brown describes in the *American Angler's Guide* published in 1849, in Connecticut, New York, and Long Island, bluefishing was "usually performed in a good-sized sailboat, with a guide who knows the ground, or by casting from the shore and drawing in alternately. The former method is most practiced, and being highly approved of by the fair sex, who often compose the best part of a fishing party, of course stamps it at once with perfection. To those ladies who have to be placed on the list as invalids, and can endure the delightful and bracing summer breeze and gentle south wind, a few days sport in the Sound with a bluefishing party will repay them for their exertions."

This outing sounds like a perfect summer idyll, but bluefish is one of the most voracious and cannibalistic fish in the sea, feeding in bloody blitzes, surrounding baitfish such as mackerel, herring, and menhaden, and gorging themselves in a feeding frenzy. One of its nicknames is the "chopper" due to its sharp teeth that have taken more than a few fingers from inexperienced fishermen. As Professor Spencer F. Baird noted in his 1874 report to the United States Fish Commission, a school of bluefish moves "like a pack of hungry wolves, destroying everything before them. Their trail is marked by fragments of fish and the stain of blood in the sea." Somehow, you'd think that the peace and quiet of a pleasant sail might be interrupted—especially for "the fair sex"—by all those sharp teeth and indiscriminate gorging.

According to Captain Steve White, who has been successfully fishing the waters from Maine to Long Island for more than fifty years: "Bluefish are strong fighting fish, in addition to being voracious eating machines making them much sought after quarry by fishermen using light tackle. It's a special treat to land one on a fly rod."

He goes on to say: "Baby bluefish or snappers are a treat for children to catch and are also fine table fare. For years, snappers sautéed in butter was a breakfast staple in Long Island. Although stronger in flavor than many fish, bluefish in the five- to ten-pound range can provide a fine meal if bled out immediately after catching and iced down. Fillets should have all of the red meat removed, as this is where the 'gamy' flavor lives. Remember to take quick care of your catch that is heading to the table so take plenty of ice in the boat when the bluefish show up this summer."

The excitement of bluefishing from *Harper's Weekly* in 1885.

STEVE WHITE'S KEEP-IT-SIMPLE BLUEFISH

Steve doesn't use recipes but cooks his catch in whatever manner appeals to him that day. "Bluefish can be baked whole, with onions and tomatoes or with a variety of garden vegetables. Skinned fillets, sautéed in butter and olive oil after being doused with seasoned flour and dipped in an egg wash is an easy way to prepare bluefish. Whatever you do, as with all fish, do not overcook!"

8 tablespoons butter, divided with 4 tablespoons cut into slices

2 pounds bluefish fillets

3 tablespoons fresh lemon juice

½ cup white wine

1 tablespoon Old Bay Seasoning or your favorite dry fish seasoning

1. Preheat oven to 350°F.

2. Grease a glass baking dish with 4 tablespoons of butter. Place fillets in baking dish and brush the fish with the lemon juice.

3. Place remaining pats of butter on the fillets and pour the white wine over. Sprinkle Old Bay over each.

4. Bake for 20 to 30 minutes until fish is just beginning to flake. Sprinkle parsley over the fish and serve with lemon wedges.

SERVES 4–6

SMOKY BARBEQUED BLUEFISH

This recipe comes from the Maine Fishermen's Wives Association, founded in 1977 in order for the wives of fishermen (there were few female fishermen in those days, which is not true today) to help their husbands increase their awareness of the industry and generally support the land-based side of fishing.

2 tablespoons vegetable oil

1 cup sour cream

⅛ teaspoon salt

2 teaspoons horseradish

1 tablespoon fresh lemon juice

3 tablespoons capers, optional

1 tablespoon dill

Pepper to taste

2 pounds bluefish fillets,
   with skin

1. Combine all ingredients well except the fish and chill.

2. Preheat grill or light charcoal. Score skin to keep fillet from curling. Brush with oil.

3. When the grill is hot, place fillets skin side down on grill about 5 inches from coals. Cover and cook for 10 to 15 minutes or until fish flakes.

4. Carefully remove fish from grill and place on a large platter and serve with sauce on the side.

SERVES 4-6

SMOKED BLUEFISH

Bluefish is an excellent fish to smoke due to its oily consistency and strong flavor, which stands up to the smoking. If you like smoked fish, you will really like smoked bluefish. Leave the skin on the fillets that you plan to smoke, as this will hold the meat together during the process. You can also freeze the fillets until you are ready to spend a few hours around your smoker.

MARINADE FOR SMOKING BLUEFISH

1 cup fruit juice such as pineapple (you can use more than one kind)

Juice of a lemon

2 tablespoons soy sauce

Fresh ground pepper, to taste

2 cloves of garlic, crushed

2 tablespoons brown sugar

1 tablespoon rice wine vinegar

Smokers have been made from old refrigerators, oil drums, and a variety of other ingenious designs but are now readily available and inexpensive, either charcoal or electric, and come with good directions. Packaged wood chips to flavor the smoke are also available if you don't have access to fruit wood branches, such as apple.

Since we are now mostly smoking for flavor and most of us have refrigeration, marinades of fruit juices, vinegars, spices, oils, wines, brown sugar, and many other ingredients are used to flavor, not preserve. There are numerous recipes for brines and marinades available both online and in print; *The Quick and Easy Art of Smoking Food* by Chris Dubbs is a good source of information.

1. Whisk all ingredients together and marinate fish for 2 to 6 hours.

2. Then smoke the fish according to directions.

MAKES 1½ CUPS MARINADE

Cod

Biologically speaking, the cod family makes up a large portion of the New England catch, since haddock, hake, and pollock are related species. But for culinary purposes, I have distinguished among the different types—they have slightly different tastes and textures—although I have indicated when one might be substituted for another in a recipe. All are firm, lean-fleshed, cold-water white fish, some of the most delicious in the world, to my taste. And when you eat a piece of cod, you are taking a bite out of New England history.

THE COD FAMILY

A reunion of the cod family would be quite a gathering. It would include haddock, hake, pollock, cusk, tomcod, and scrod, along with such preparations as salt cod and finnan haddie.

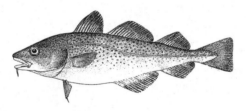

The Atlantic cod is, of course, the pater familias, and some of the rest of the family suffer by comparison.

Haddock is the second most popular of the cod family. It closely resembles the cod, although is usually gray with a black patch on its side; the cod has a brownish cast. From a culinary point of view, haddock is almost interchangeable with cod, although it's thought to be less appropriate for salting. Haddock is, however, the preferred fish for finnan haddie, which is split, smoked haddock; *haddie* is Scottish slang for "haddock."

Hake's problem, at least in the United States, is that it needs better publicity. Oddly enough, this has been tried by renaming the hake to something that might sound more appealing, including whiting, whitefish, Pacific whiting, and ling. Nothing has really worked, and typically the price of hake is about half that of cod. The meat is much like cod, though somewhat coarser textured.

In Europe hake is more highly regarded and appears under its own name on menus at expensive restaurants. At the same time, Gorton's excellent *Fish Glossary* says that hake "provides many countries with a good inexpensive source of protein." A noble calling to be sure, but not haute cuisine.

Codfishing from a dory in 1902. These dories were carried to the fishing grounds aboard schooners like the *L. A. Dunton*.

Pollock is the species of choice for frozen fish, fish sticks, and fish-and-chips—but that doesn't mean that it isn't a good substitute for cod. Indeed, this common usage may be only a reflection of tradition and the fact that pollock is still abundant and easier to catch than cod. Pollock flesh is firm and may be grayer than cod. Its high fat content lends a slightly stronger taste than cod. Pollock are popular with recreational fishermen, as they are caught in shallower waters than cod and are stronger fighters. Cod, on the other hand, seem to take a more fatalistic view of being caught by rod and reel.

Cusk is the odd-looking member of the family, with its full-length dorsal fin and small eyes. It's becoming more popular as a culinary substitute for the more expensive cod, but much of the catch is still salted or goes into frozen food as "white fish."

The tomcod looks like an immature cod but is actually a smaller variety—most are less than twelve inches long. Tomcod are voracious eaters and provide good sport for inshore anglers. They're highly prized for their delicate flavor.

Although a popular New England menu item, *scrod* is really only a culinary term for a young member of the cod family. It could be any one of the above species.

"This is good old Boston,
The home of the bean and the cod,
Where the Lowells talk to the Cabots
And the Cabots talk only to God."

—JOHN COLLINS BOSSIDY

FISH CHOWDER

I include this chowder recipe in the cod chapter because cod—given its traditional abundance—has long been a popular chowder fish. You could, however, use any firm white-fleshed fish, including haddock or cusk. I tend to prefer these to halibut (too expensive for chowder, in my view), and to flounder and sole, which are a bit too delicate for the soup pot. At any rate, fish chowder recipes seem to have changed very little over the years.

2 slices thick-cut bacon, or
    2 tablespoons diced salt pork
5 medium potatoes, cut into
    ½-inch chunks
1 large onion, chopped
2 cups fish stock or water
1½ pounds cod, cut into 1-inch
    pieces
1 pint light cream
1 12-ounce can evaporated
    skimmed milk
Salt and pepper, to taste
Butter, for serving

1. In a frying pan, cook the bacon or salt pork until it's browned and its fat is rendered. Pour off all but 2 tablespoons of fat.

2. Add the potatoes and onion to the pan and cook in the fat until the onion is translucent. Add fish stock or water to cover and simmer for 10 minutes.

3. Add the cod and simmer for another 5 to 10 minutes, or until the fish is cooked through.

4. Add the cream and evaporated milk and heat through. Season to taste. Serve very hot with a dab of butter added to each bowl, if desired.

SERVES 6-8

KEDGEREE

This is an old-time recipe for cod that probably originated with English settlers and fishermen. It is adapted for today's cooks in *A Taste of History: 19th Century Food of Mystic Seaport.*

2 tablespoons butter

2 tablespoons flour

2 cups milk

4 finely chopped hard-boiled egg
 yolks (whites, optional)

Salt and pepper, to taste

2 cups cooked white rice

1 cup cooked, flaked codfish

1. Preheat the oven to 350°F.

2. Make a white sauce: Melt the butter in a saucepan over medium heat. Whisk in the flour and cook until a smooth paste forms. Whisk in the milk and stir until thickened. Add the yolks, salt, and pepper.

3. Add the cooked rice and fish, and toss until well blended. Put into a greased casserole dish or baking pan. (Options: Season with nutmeg or mace; top with buttered cracker crumbs.)

4. Bake until hot and bubbling.

SERVES 6-8

ROAST COD WITH POTATO-HORSERADISH CRUST

I love this combination of flavors. It's not hard to make, but turn the fish carefully to keep the crust intact.

2 medium baking potatoes, grated

1 shallot, finely minced

1 egg white, beaten

2 tablespoons horseradish

Salt and pepper, to taste

1½ pounds cod fillets, divided into 4 portions

2 tablespoons mayonnaise

1 tablespoon vegetable oil

1. Preheat the oven to 425°F.

2. In a clean dish towel, squeeze any excess liquid from the grated potatoes. In a small bowl, combine the potatoes, shallot, egg white, and horseradish. Mix well.

3. Salt and pepper the cod to taste. Spread the mayonnaise on the cod fillets and top with the potato mixture.

4. Heat the oil in a frying pan, and carefully place the cod fillets, potato-side down, into the pan. Fry until the potatoes are golden.

5. Place the fish potato-side up in a baking dish, and bake for 10 to 12 minutes or until the fish is opaque and flaky.

SERVES 4

OVEN-ROASTED COD

WITH LOBSTER, CORN, POTATO, AND CREAM

This wonderful entree from chef Valerie Lareau of Robert's Maine Grill in Kittery, Maine, takes classic New England ingredients and gives them a simple but elegant spin.

1 russet potato

½ cup rendered duck fat or
   bacon fat

Pinch of sea salt

Pinch of black pepper

1 1½-pound lobster, cooked

1 ear corn

12 ounces fresh cod fillets, cut
   into 2 portions

½ cup heavy cream

1. Preheat the oven to 400°F. Shred the potato and hold in a bowl of cold water.

2. Melt the duck fat or bacon fat in a heavy skillet.

3. Drain the potato and squeeze out any excess water. Spread evenly in the hot skillet and let brown. Salt and pepper lightly. When it's brown, drain on a paper towel.

4. Pick the meat out of the cooked lobster and slice.

5. Shuck the corn. Cut the kernels from the cob and set aside.

6. Place the cod portions in an ovenproof pan; salt and pepper to taste. Lay the potato, corn, and lobster loosely on top of the fish, then add the heavy cream to the pan. Bake for 15 minutes or until just opaque and flaky.

SERVES 2

BAKED COD WITH SHALLOTS AND LEMON

This is a homey recipe that has been around for some time in various incarnations. I like it because it doesn't need a lot of exotic ingredients and is simple and quick.

1 cup mayonnaise

½ cup grated Parmesan cheese

4 tablespoons white Worcestershire sauce

3 tablespoons fresh lemon juice

Salt and pepper, to taste

2 pounds cod fillets

1 lemon, thinly sliced

2 shallots, thinly sliced

1. Preheat the oven to 400°F.

2. Mix the mayonnaise, Parmesan, Worcestershire, and lemon juice in a small bowl. Salt and pepper the fish to taste, then spread the cheese mixture atop the cod fillets.

3. Place three or four slices of shallots and of lemon on top of the mixture. Bake the cod for 20 minutes or until it's opaque and flakes easily.

SERVES 6

THE SACRED COD

Codfish occupies such an important place in New England history that since the eighteenth century (except when it was stolen by some Harvard students in 1933 as a prank), a five-foot-long carved wooden cod has hung over the entrance to the chamber of the Massachusetts House of Representatives. It's known as The Sacred Cod.

In 1784 John Rowe, a Boston native and Massachusetts representative, proposed the following motion: "That leave might be given to hang up the representation of a cod fish in the room where the House sit[s], as a memorial of the importance of the Cod-Fishery to the welfare of the Commonwealth. . . ." The carved cod was installed and was later moved to the "new" State House building in 1798.

SALT COD

Salt cod is one of the great examples of necessity being the mother of virtue. The original function of salting cod—or other fish, for that matter—was to preserve it for future use. Fresh fish has a very short shelf life, and even iced fish (ice being itself a precious commodity before electricity) doesn't last very long. Salted and dried fish, however, lasted the weeks and months it took to get from the fishing grounds in the New World back to Europe on a sailing vessel and then to market.

The first Europeans who came to New England caught cod, salted it, dried it on wooden racks ("flakes"), and sailed it back to Europe. At first they came in the spring and returned with their salted cod in the fall. In the mid-1600s fishermen began to winter over in places like the Isles of Shoals, New Hampshire. These fishermen became the first European inhabitants of New England. All for salt cod.

A salt cod aboard the four-masted bark *Peking* in 1929.

What is amazing about salt cod now, even in the age of refrigeration and freezing, is that it has much more than a nostalgic place in many cuisines. Its flavor and texture continue to be highly valued long after its original purpose has disappeared.

The basics of salting cod are quite simple. The cleaned fish is packed with coarse salt, layer upon layer, either in a barrel or in the open air. The weight of the many layers of salt and cod helps force out more of the moisture. After ten days to three weeks, depending upon temperature and humidity, any loose salt and dirt is removed, and

A good-size fish taken aboard the *L. A. Dunton* in the 1920s.

the salted cod is set on flakes to dry. The waterfront of fishing towns used to be dominated by salt flakes. You can see a small section of flakes today at Mystic Seaport.

The air-drying fish are sometimes shaded against too much sun. In New England, however, they're more often covered by tarps against rain and fog.

The fascinating short film *A Hard Racket for Living*—made in 1948 and available for view on the Internet—shows the cod-salting process in Newfoundland and Labrador.

For connoisseurs of salt cod, a number of different cure recipes are available, ranging from a mild cure with relatively low salt content to a more intense version ("high cured") with double the amount of salt. A mild-cured fish is usually somewhat flexible and off-white in color. The rock-hard salt cod we usually see in our supermarkets is high cured.

If salt cod is not available in your area, you can approximate a mild cure by packing a cleaned cod in coarse salt (using a glass container) and leaving it in the fridge for about three days—or you can use the same technique for seven to ten days in the open air. Every few days, check to see that there are no airspaces between the salted fish.

TRADITIONAL JAMAICAN SALT COD

This recipe appeared in the *Jamaica Cookery Book* in 1893 and is still considered one of the national dishes of Jamaica. It's the kind of dish that probably provided sustenance to slaves laboring in the cane fields, who were fed inferior salted cod caught in the waters off New England.

Ackee is a tropical fruit with texture resembling scrambled eggs. The flesh of the seedpods is edible when ripe (indeed, the seeds are toxic, as the cookbook writer points out) and has a mild sweetness that contrasts with the saltiness of the cod. The salt cod would have been soaked in several changes of water to make it possible to cook.

1 pound of salt fish

The fruit of 12 ackee pods

Lard

Butter

Black pepper

Soak the salt fish overnight. Put it on to boil in cold water, otherwise it hardens; throw off the first water and put it on again to boil. Carefully pick the ackees free from all red inside, which is dangerous, and boil them for about 20 minutes; add them to the salt fish, which is then cut in small pieces; add some lard, butter and pepper. Some prefer the salt fish and ackees mashed together and the melted lard and butter poured over the top.

COD CAKES WITH CHILI-LIME MAYONNAISE

This is an updated twist on a very old recipe. Salt cod and potatoes could historically be kept for a long period of time, making this a popular combination. You could also make this with leftover fresh cod and leftover mashed potatoes.

1 pound salt cod

1 whole lime, sliced

2 medium potatoes

2 cloves garlic, sliced

4 tablespoons olive oil, divided

⅓ cup diced bell pepper

½ cup diced scallions

Zest of 1 whole lime

Juice of 1 lime

1 teaspoon chili-garlic sauce

½ cup good-quality mayonnaise

⅓ cup plain yogurt

1. First, prepare the salt cod for cooking: Brush any extra salt off the cod fillets and rinse them well under running water. Place them in a glass dish and cover with water. Refrigerate for 24 hours, rinsing and changing the water three times during that period.

2. Rinse one last time and place in a large saucepan with a cover. Slice 1 lime into wedges and place atop the fillets.

3. Add water to cover. Simmer, covered, for 8 to 10 minutes or until the fish flakes easily in your hands.

4. Next, make the fish cakes: Peel and chop the potatoes. Place them in a saucepan and add the sliced garlic. Simmer for 15 minutes or until the potatoes are soft. Drain thoroughly and mash.

5. In a sauté pan, heat 1 tablespoon of the olive oil. Add the pepper and scallions and sauté until just soft.

6. In a bowl, combine the cod, mashed potatoes, and sautéed vegetables; mix well. The mixture should be sticky enough to form into cakes with your hands. Form into patties or cakes about 3 inches in diameter for an entree, or 1 inch for hors d'oeuvre size.

7. Heat another tablespoon of the olive oil in a frying pan and fry the cakes until golden brown on each side, adding more oil as necessary. Drain on paper towels and keep warm.

8. Finally, make the mayonnaise: Combine the lime zest, lime juice, chili-garlic sauce, mayonnaise, and yogurt in a nonreactive bowl. Chill and serve with the cod cakes.

MAKES 8 FISH CAKES OR 24 HORS D'OEUVRE PORTIONS

Flounder

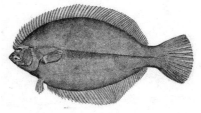

Flounder are part of a large family of flatfish that are found in both the Atlantic and the Pacific. They are closely related to other flatfish, including the largest bottom dweller, halibut, and the tiny, delicate sand dabs that may weigh as little as six ounces. But there's a good deal of confusion when it comes to identifying flounder, as opposed to sole, dab, or plaice. Suffice it to say they are all delicious and lend themselves to a wide variety of cooking methods.

In New England the most common species are winter flounder—which, to continue the confusion, is often marketed as lemon sole—and summer flounder, also known as fluke. Summer flounder are found in sandy harbors and bays and come in a variety of mottled browns and grays. They can camouflage themselves to some degree to blend in with their environment.

Winter flounder range from Labrador to the coasts of the Carolinas, but they're most common along the North Atlantic. According to Captain Dave, a Boston-based charter captain, angler, and saltwater fish expert: "In New England, flounder reproduce in estuaries from January to May, with peak activity in February and March when the water temperatures are the coldest of the year. Evidence suggests that individual fish return for many years to the same site to spawn. . . ." And Captain Dave is no stranger to the culinary aspects of flounder. As he says: "Few fish lend themselves to more imaginative dishes as does winter flounder. Its texture and delicate flavor are well suited to sauces, spices, fruit, vegetables, and other seafood. Few things can be mixed with so many things and still stand out." In fact, *Larousse Gastronomique*, the bible of classic French cooking, lists no fewer than twenty-six preparations for sole. I've only included a few in this chapter, but try inventing your own sauces, seasoning blends, and stuffings. It's hard to go wrong.

FISHING FOR DOORMATS

One of my favorite summer pastimes when I was a little girl was flounder fishing. You hear flounder referred to as doormats, for their tendency to just sit on the ocean floor like, well, a doormat. It wasn't exactly sportfishing—more just a matter of pulling them off the bottom. We'd anchor the skiff fifty yards or so offshore and drop anchor. I had my own handline with one small hook and a lead weight attached. I can still remember the smell of the tar used to coat the line so it wouldn't rot away.

If we were fishing with pieces of clams, I could bait my own hook, but when it came to seaworms, it was a job for Dad. (I bait my own hook these days, but truth be told I'd still rather have someone else do it.) Then it was a matter of choosing which side of the boat to fish on. Most of the time we could see the bottom, and once our eyes adjusted we'd sometimes catch the slight sandy motion of a flounder rippling across the seafloor. We plunked the bait in front of the fish until he decided it was his next meal.

Then he became our next meal—home to Mom, who never complained about the cleaning and gutting. She'd serve our flounder pan-fried, sometimes with homemade french fries and always with tartar sauce. On a good day we'd bring home six or eight fish—a feast for our small family. I still think that if anyone who claims they don't like fish had it this fresh and this deliciously prepared, they'd become converts.

LEMON SOLE AMANDINE
WITH WHITE GRAPES AND TARRAGON

This recipe brings together two of the classic French preparations: Sole Veronique and Sole Amandine. It's a signature dish of chef Gordon Breidenbach, owner of Scandia Restaurant in Amesbury, Massachusetts.

FOR THE SAUCE

1 cup green seedless grapes

1 teaspoon fresh tarragon

1 tablespoon honey

1½ cups white wine

FOR THE SOLE

3 teaspoons unsalted butter, divided

1 teaspoon olive oil

4 sole or flounder fillets, 4–5 ounces each

1 tablespoon flour, seasoned to taste with salt and pepper

1 egg beaten with ⅓ cup milk

2 ounces slivered almonds

1 teaspoon chopped parsley

½ teaspoon chopped tarragon

1. Make the Sauce: Combine all the ingredients and bring the mixture to a boil. Remove from the heat and cover. You can make this ahead of time and refrigerate until ready to use.

2. Make the Sole: Melt 1 teaspoon of the butter in a skillet, and add the olive oil.

3. Dredge the flounder in the seasoned flour and coat with the egg mixture. Combine the almonds, parsley, and tarragon and top each fillet with this mixture.

4. Place the fillets in the skillet with this side up for 1 to 2 minutes, until almost cooked through. Carefully turn them over to brown the fillets on other side for a minute or so. Flip again, spoon some of the grapes on top, and keep warm,

5. Add 5 tablespoons of the grape liquid to the pan along with remaining 2 teaspoons of butter. Cook over moderate heat until the sauce is smooth. Spoon over the fillets and serve.

SERVES 4-6

CRAB-STUFFED FLOUNDER ROULADES

This is a quick and easy preparation that is definitely good enough for a dinner party.

12 ounces fresh or frozen crabmeat

1 tablespoon mayonnaise

1 tablespoon diced shallot

1 tablespoon sliced fresh chives

4 flounder fillets, 4–5 ounces each

2 tablespoons olive oil

Salt and pepper, to taste

1. Preheat the oven to 450°F.

2. In a bowl, combine the crabmeat, mayonnaise, shallot, and chives.

3. Cut the flounder fillets in half lengthwise on their side, cut side down. Place a tablespoon or more of the crab mixture on each strip and roll up.

4. Brush the fish with olive oil and season with salt and pepper.

5. Bake for 8 to 10 minutes or until the fish is just cooked through and flakes easily.

SERVES 2

TO MAKE A FLOUNDER PIE

"Gut some flounders, wash them clean, dry them in a cloth, just boil them, cut off the meat clean, from the bones, lay a good crust over the dish and lay a little fresh butter in the bottom, and on that the fish; season with salt and pepper to your mind. Boil the bones in the water your fish was boiled in, with a little bit of horse-raddish, a little parsley, a very little bit of lemon-peel and a crust of bread. Boil it till there is just enough liquor for the pie then strain it, and put it in your pie; put on the top-crust and bake it."

The Art of Cookery Made Plain and Easy,
"Excelling any Thing of the Kind ever yet published,"
by Mrs. Glasse (1776)

FLOUNDER BONNE FEMME

This is one of the classic French preparations of sole. I made this dish for my then-husband-to-be on one of our first dates, using a Julia Child recipe. Maybe I was subconsciously trying to tell him I was indeed a bonne femme—or maybe it's just that I like mushrooms so much. Anyway, here's my little twist on the classic, using a variety of mushrooms and herbs.

4 tablespoons butter, divided

2 tablespoons finely chopped shallots

1 pound mixed exotic mushrooms, sliced (porcini, oyster, shiitake, cremini, or a mixture of your favorites)

3 pounds flounder fillets

1½ cups dry white wine

1 tablespoon fresh lemon juice

1 tablespoon chopped parsley

1 tablespoon chopped fresh summer savory, tarragon, or your favorite herbs

1 teaspoon salt, plus more to taste

¼ teaspoon white pepper, plus more to taste

1½ tablespoons flour

1 cup heavy cream

1. Heat 2 tablespoons of the butter in a sauté pan. Add the shallots and mushrooms and cook until they begin to soften.

2. Fold the fillets into thirds and place in the pan. Add wine to just cover the fillets. Add the lemon juice, parsley, fresh herbs, salt, and pepper.

3. Cover the pan with a circle of waxed paper with a small vent hole cut in the middle. Bring to a boil. Reduce the heat and simmer for 3 minutes. Remove the fillets to a platter and keep them warm; leave the wine-mushroom mixture in the pan.

4. Blend the flour and 1 tablespoon of the butter into a paste.

5. Turn up the heat under the pan and reduce the wine-mushroom mixture by half. Add the flour-butter paste, whisking until thick and smooth. Add the cream, bring to a boil, and remove from the heat. Season to taste with salt and pepper.

6. Add the remaining butter a little at a time, shaking the pan gently to gradually melt it. Pour over the fish and glaze under a broiler until golden. Serve immediately.

SERVES 6

PAN-FRIED FLOUNDER WITH BROWN SAGE BUTTER

Brown butter with sage is a classic Italian "sauce" for pasta—often ravioli or other pasta stuffed with squash or pumpkin—that is simple and elegant, and lets the flavors of the dish shine through. That's why I like this so much over flounder. Oven-roasted winter squash would make a nice side dish.

½ cup flour

1 teaspoon sea salt

½ teaspoon white pepper

2 tablespoons butter, divided

1 tablespoon olive oil

½ cup fresh sage leaves, washed
  and dried

1 clove garlic, minced

1 pound flounder fillets

⅓ cup white wine

1. Combine the flour, salt, and pepper on a plate.

2. Heat 1 tablespoon of the butter, along with the oil, in a large sauté pan. Add the sage leaves and fry until crisp. Remove from the pan and drain on paper towels.

3. Add the garlic to the pan and sauté for 1 minute over medium heat.

4. Dredge the flounder fillets in the flour mixture and add to the pan. Sauté for 1 to 2 minutes over medium-high heat or until golden brown on each side. Remove the fillets and keep them warm. Add the remaining butter and cook until just slightly colored. Add the wine to the pan and cook for 1 minute more.

5. Serve the fillets drizzled with pan juices, with the sage leaves crumbled over the top.

SERVES 2-4

Haddock

Biologically speaking, haddock is a part of the cod family, as are pollock, hake, tomcod, and other species noted in the cod chapter. But for culinary purposes, haddock is such a delicious and popular fish that I decided to give it its own section in *Mystic Seafood*.

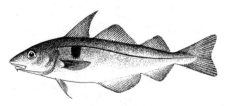

Haddock is now one of America's favorite fish, found in a vast number of New England restaurants from the humblest fried-food joint to top-notch restaurants. In the eighteenth and nineteenth centuries, however, haddock was considered only a poor relation of cod—primarily because it wasn't as good a salted fish. Fresh haddock was recognized for its wonderful flavor and texture, but was a smaller fishery. In the latter half of the nineteenth century, as fresh fish grew more popular than salted, haddock began to be fully appreciated. As its following grew, it became available smoked as finnan haddie, a popular food with the English and Scottish immigrants in the Canadian Maritime provinces, since finnan haddie is a much-loved British dish. The other factor was that haddock were, and are, best caught on a line. Haddock caught in the nets used to catch cod just didn't hold up as well.

The good news is that haddock has finally earned its due respect as a foodstuff. The bad news is that it has become so popular, stocks in the Atlantic have been much depleted. In fact, between 1977 and 1985 the haddock fishery in New England declined by more than 80 percent. The unpredictable catch from year to year is a factor in the survival of young haddock, which are also very popular dining choices for their cousins cod and pollock. Not only that but, according to the Massachusetts Division of Marine Fisheries: "The number of larvae that survive in a given year is often chiefly determined by their location when they are ready to become bottom dwellers. If the currents in which they have been suspended have carried them far offshore from the continental shelf, few larvae will survive. Haddock populations characteristically suffer through extended series of years when few fish survive early life stages."

Haddock range all the way across the Atlantic, from the American side to the European. In summer they range from the southern part of the Grand Banks to Cape Cod. In the colder months they can be found as far south as Cape Hatteras, North Carolina. You can tell a haddock from other members of the cod family by its three dorsal fins and a long black stripe running the length of the fish. The upper part of the fish is a violet-gray shade, gradually fading to a white underbelly.

OVEN-"FRIED" FISH-AND-CHIPS

I love fish-and-chips, but my waistline does not. This is a lighter version based on a method of cooking fish developed by Evalene Spencer of the U.S. Bureau of Fisheries in 1934, according to the *Encyclopedia of Fish Cookery.* You'll need a good hot oven—the temperature should get up to 500°F.

1 tablespoon vegetable oil

1 tablespoon fine sea salt

³/₄ cup milk

Finely sifted Italian flavored
    bread crumbs

2 teaspoons paprika, divided

2 pounds haddock fillets, cut into
    4 pieces

6 medium russet potatoes, cut
    lengthwise into eighths and
    patted dry

Nonstick cooking spray

1 tablespoon coarse sea salt

Lemon wedges, for serving

Tartar sauce, for serving

1. Preheat the oven to 500°F. Grease a baking dish with vegetable oil.

2. In a bowl, stir the fine salt into the milk until dissolved. Place this to the left of your work area.

3. Combine the bread crumbs and 1 teaspoon of the paprika on a plate or in a shallow bowl. Place this to the right of your work area.

4. Using one hand to dip the fish into the salted milk, and the other hand for the dry ingredients, dip each piece of haddock into the milk, and then roll it gently in the crumbs with your dry hand. Place on a baking dish.

5. Add the potatoes to the baking dish. Spray everything generously with nonstick spray. Sprinkle the coarse salt and remaining paprika on the potatoes and bake for 10 minutes, turning the fish gently after 5 minutes and stirring the potatoes. Serve hot with lemon wedges and Tartar Sauce (see recipe on the following page) if you like.

SERVES 4

TARTAR SAUCE

This classic sauce for seafood has evolved over the years. The 1896 *Boston Cooking School Cookbook* called for vinegar, lemon juice, Worcestershire sauce, and butter. By 1939 Imogene Wolcott's *New England Yankee Cookbook* offered a recipe similar to the one below. In keeping with trying to cut down on the fat and calories, I like to lighten up tartar sauce using reduced-fat mayonnaise.

1 cup reduced-fat mayonnaise

1 tablespoon minced onion

2 tablespoons sweet pickle relish

1 tablespoon fresh lemon juice

Pinch of Old Bay Seasoning

Salt and pepper, to taste

Combine all the ingredients in a bowl and refrigerate for at least an hour before using. This is great with any fried or oven-"fried" fish.

> "Give me a platter of choice finnan haddie,
> freshly cooked in its bath of water and milk,
> add melted butter, a slice or two of hot toast,
> a pot of steaming Darjeeling tea,
> and you may tell the butler to dispense with
> the caviar, truffles, and nightingales' tongues."
>
> **—CRAIG CLAIBORNE**

SMOKY HADDOCK CHOWDER

Finnan haddie gives this chowder a smoky flavor. You could also add a bit of finnan haddie to the recipe for Cod Cakes with Chili-Lime Mayonnaise on (in the chapter on cod) to give them a similar appeal.

1 slice thick-cut bacon, or
    1 tablespoon diced salt pork

¼ pound finnan haddie or
    smoked haddock

1 large onion, chopped

5 medium potatoes, cut into
    ½-inch chunks

2 cups fish stock or water

1¼ pounds cod or haddock, cut
    into 1-inch pieces

1 pint (2 cups) light cream

1 12-ounce can evaporated
    skimmed milk

Salt and pepper, to taste

Butter, for serving

1. In a frying pan, cook the bacon or salt pork until it's brown and the fat is rendered. Pour off all but 1 tablespoon of the fat.

2. Add the finnan haddie, onion, and potatoes to the pan and cook in the bacon fat until the onion is translucent. Add fish stock or water to cover and simmer for 10 minutes. Flake the finnan haddie with a fork.

3. Add the cod or haddock and simmer for another 5 to 10 minutes or until the fish is cooked through. Separate the fish into pieces.

4. Add the cream and evaporated milk and heat through. Season to taste. Serve very hot with a dab of butter added to each bowl, if desired.

SERVES 6

Alfred Jones' Sons brand canned finnan haddie—smoked haddock.

BAKED HADDOCK WITH CRUMB TOPPING

Baked haddock is probably the most common fish preparation in New England restaurants. It's nothing fancy, but really lets the flavors of a great piece of haddock shine through.

1 cup dry stuffing mix, such as
  Pepperidge Farm Herb Seasoned Stuffing mix
Juice of 1 lemon
4 tablespoons butter, melted
Salt and pepper, to taste
2 pounds haddock fillets, cut into
  6 pieces

1. Preheat the oven to 450°F.

2. Combine the stuffing mix, lemon juice, and melted butter.

3. Salt and pepper the fillets to taste and press equal amounts of topping onto each.

4. Bake for 10 minutes or until the fish flakes easily and the topping is crisp and brown.

SERVES 6

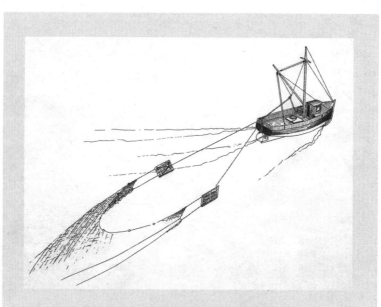

A western-rig dragger (the pilothouse is forward). The "doors" hold the net open as the boat drags it through the water.

Halibut

Halibut seem to have inspired many legends over the years, possibly because among the flatfish—which include flounder, sole, plaice, and turbot—they are by far the largest.

Pre-Christian Norwegians regarded the halibut as a god-like fish, serious and wise. To this day the species is associated with feast days in Norway. In the New World many of the halibut legends concern its size and vast appetite. Atlantic halibut (slightly different from the Pacific halibut) grow to about 700 pounds and as much as nine feet long, although most of the halibut caught these days are 50 to 100 pounds.

Captain John Smith, the seventeenth-century explorer, never shy about extolling the virtues of New England, wrote, "There is a large sized fish called the Hallibut, or Turbot: some are taken so bigg that that two men have much a doe to hall them into the boate: but there is such a plenty, that the fishermen onlye eat the heads & finnes, and throw away the bodies."

By the nineteenth century inshore halibut stocks were diminishing. In 1876 it was a newsworthy event when some Noank, Connecticut, fishermen caught a few halibut about eight miles from Mystic.

Offshore, large halibut were still being taken, and fishermen and naturalists seemed to delight in the astounding contents of their stomachs: live lobsters, a block of wood "a cubic foot in dimensions," an accordion key, pieces of iron, and "a large piece of floe ice."

In the *Fisheries and Fishery Industry of the United States, 1884*, Captain Collins, a halibut fisherman out of Gloucester, Massachusetts, documented (or at least claimed to have witnessed) some truly bizarre halibut behavior. "The man at the

This halibut schooner is anchored on the fishing grounds as the crew cuts bait and baits the lines of hooks called trawls.

wheel sang out that he saw a Halibut flapping its tale about a quarter of a mile off our starboard quarter. I looked through the spy-glass, and his statement was soon verified by the second appearance of the tail. We hove out a dory, and two men went in her, taking with them a pair of gaff-hooks. They soon returned bringing with them not only the Halibut, which was a fine one, of about seventy pounds' weight, but a small codfish which it had been trying to kill by striking it with its tail. The codfish was quite exhausted by the repeated blows, and did not attempt to escape after its enemy had been captured. The Halibut was so completely engaged in pursuit of the codfish that it paid no attention to the dory, and was easily captured."

Throughout the twentieth century the halibut catch continued to decline, although it has recovered somewhat in recent years. Most halibut purchased in the United States comes from Canada and has been caught on deep-water longlines, baited hooks that lie on the seafloor. Halibut are being farmed in Maine and in Norway, with some recent experiments raising them in pens off the New Hampshire coast.

Chicken halibut (smaller and younger) are preferred, because whale halibut can be firmer and drier. The flesh is white and delicately flavored. You may be able to find the highly prized halibut cheeks in some gourmet fish markets.

NOTHING BUT THE BEST

One of the many wonderful experiences we had while working on this book was a visit to the famous Boston Fish Pier, built in 1912. This is home to numerous wholesale purveyors of seafood, but most will sell to the public retail—cash on the barrelhead.

A standout on the pier is Sunny's Seafood, which provided us with some incredible raw materials: striped bass (a whole side freshly cut), halibut, and skate that were just as fresh as they come. The place is immaculate and their expertise impressive.

Sunny's has been around since 1989 and is owned by the Dulock family. Since its inception, Sunny's has practiced sustainable fisheries management, buying only from fishing boats that use the most environmentally sound methods of catching fish. Sunny's buys only from small "day boat" fishing vessels to ensure the freshest seafood with the lowest damaging by catch, and serves some of the top restaurants and retailers in the area.

CEVICHE (OR SEVICHE)

Ceviche is a popular means of "cooking" fish without heat, using citrus and other seasoning. It originated in South America and can be used with a wide variety of fish and shellfish. Shrimp and scallops are particularly delicious. I sampled a version in Key West, Florida, that included conch. Carleton Mitchell, sailor, adventurer, writer, and longtime friend of Mystic Seaport, writes about an exotic version of seviche—or what he calls *poisson cru*—in his memoir *The Winds Call* about his adventures at sea:

> *Poisson cru*—called *e i'a ota* in Tahitian, plain "raw fish" in English—had become my favorite Polynesian dish. Nothing is more delicious. Nor is it raw, except in the sense it is not cooked by heat. Now at last I was to see it made, as Terri took over the string Sam lifted aboard.
>
> Almost any sort of fish may be used, although bonito is considered best by Tahitians. After cleaning, scaling and dicing into small cubes, it was put in a bowl, and the juice of perhaps a dozen limes squeezed over—enough to thoroughly dampen the flesh. Terri anointed a layer, salted it generously and turned it with a fork, making sure none was missed. Onions were sliced in, and given a thorough tossing to mix. The bowl was covered to marinate. Thirty minutes is sufficient to cook to the taste of a true convert; after an hour the meat is done enough for almost anyone. It has the taste and texture of cooked fish, and the flavor is not strong. Excess juice is drained off and salad ingredients added—sliced tomatoes, more chopped onions, diced carrot, halved hard boiled egg, lettuce—none or all as fancy dictates. Ideally, milk from pressed coconut meat should be poured over just before serving, but this is not essential.

HALIBUT SEVICHE

This wonderful halibut seviche comes from chef Leo Bushey of Acqua Oyster Bar in Vernon, Connecticut. Chef Leo is a member of the prestigious Les Amis d'Escoffier Society and a standing member of the James Beard Foundation. Acqua Oyster Bar was voted Connecticut's Best New Restaurant in 2005.

1 medium yellow onion, peeled

2 cups fresh-squeezed lime juice

¼ cup red wine vinegar

1 tablespoon chopped fresh
  garlic

1 pound halibut, thinly sliced

Sea salt and cracked pepper,
  to taste

1 cup plum tomatoes, chopped

1 cup green pepper, diced

1 cup yellow pepper, diced

1 cup red pepper, diced

1 small bunch cilantro, washed
  and chopped

1 cup capers

1. Grate the onion into a glass or nonreactive bowl, reserving any juice. Add the lime juice, vinegar, and garlic.

2. Add the halibut and toss well. Add sea salt and cracked pepper to taste. Refrigerate overnight.

3. When you're ready to serve, drain off excess marinade, toss in tomatoes, peppers, cilantro, and capers. Serve well chilled.

SERVES 4

"If you get tired of the whole thing, you can slice almost any fine-grained fish in thin pieces, cover them with lemon or lime juice, and find them cooked in four hours without aid of stove or fire."

—*HOW TO COOK A WOLF* BY M. F. K. FISHER

OIL-POACHED HALIBUT
WITH SUN-DRIED TOMATO COULIS

You would think that poaching fish in oil would result in a greasy fish, but the result is actually a buttery tenderness that melts in your mouth.

3 cups olive oil

3 cups vegetable oil

1 head garlic

1½ pounds halibut fillets

1 cup sun-dried tomatoes in oil

1 tablespoon balsamic vinegar

1 teaspoon sea salt

½ cup white wine

½ cup fish or chicken stock

Salt and pepper, to taste

¼ cup white truffle oil

1. In a deep pan large enough to hold all the fish without crowding, combine the oils and begin to warm them over low heat.

2. Separate the cloves of garlic from the head and rub off any loose, papery skin—but do not peel. Add the garlic cloves to the oil.

3. Slowly bring the oil up to about 150°F, letting the garlic cook in it; this should take about 10 minutes.

4. Add the halibut and poach gently for 10 to 12 minutes, keeping the oil at about 150°F. When the fish is just cooked through and flakes nicely, remove the garlic and halibut from the oil. Keep the halibut warm.

5. Peel the garlic cloves and add them to a food processor. Add the sun-dried tomatoes, vinegar, sea salt, ⅓ cup of the poaching oil, wine, and the stock. Process to a sauce consistency.

6. Season the fish with salt and pepper and serve with the sun-dried tomato coulis. Drizzle truffle oil over just before serving.

SERVE 4-6

GRILLED HALIBUT
WITH NECTARINE-POBLANO SALSA

I love to grill fish any time of year, but when fish is fresh and plentiful in summer, it makes for a wonderful, simple warm-weather meal.

1 ripe but firm nectarine, seeded
   and chopped

2 medium ripe tomatoes, seeded
   and chopped

½ red bell pepper, finely
   chopped

½ red onion, finely chopped

½ poblano chile, minced

Juice of 1 lime

2 teaspoons soy sauce

1 tablespoon rice wine vinegar

3 tablespoons extra-virgin olive
   oil, divided

1½ pounds halibut steaks

Sea salt and fresh pepper,
   to taste

1. Preheat a gas grill, or light the charcoal.

2. In a nonreactive bowl, combine all the ingredients except 1 tablespoon of the olive oil, the halibut, and the salt and pepper. Cover and refrigerate, letting the salsa sit for at least 1 hour or up to 4.

3. Brush the halibut steaks with the remaining olive oil and season with salt and pepper. Grill over high heat for 4 to 5 minutes on each side or until opaque and flaky. Serve with the salsa on the side.

SERVES 4-6

Eating aboard a fishing vessel at sea can be difficult. The ship rolls, the plates slide back and forth, and soup threatens to slop out of the bowls.

Mackerel

"Mackerel scales and mare's tails make lofty ships carry low sails." This sailor's weather adage refers to the clouds that resemble the scales that run down the sides of the Atlantic mackerel and the plumelike clouds that look like horse's tails. They portend strong winds.

This plentiful fish was once a mainstay of New England commercial fishing, and while there is still a commercial mackerel fishery, using chiefly purse seines and trawls, the species' popularity has been somewhat eclipsed. Mackerel are a common catch for recreational fishermen, as the species is found near shore in the summer months and is easily caught with rod and reel. Mackerel travel in large schools and appear in Atlantic coastal waters in spring. They average about a pound but can run up to two pounds. Unlike more overfished species, there are few, if any restrictions for anglers.

Before 1870 virtually all the mackerel that was caught was salted aboard ship and often referred to as "Boston mackerel." Salting made sense: A very oily fish, mackerel spoils easily. In the days before icing or canning was possible, the catch would not have made it to the table before developing an off-taste. This short shelf life has given mackerel a bad rap, in my view, as fresh-caught mackerel cooked over hot coals are a real summer treat. There was a boom in mackerel fishing in the late 1800s, but the fishery—and demand—have come and gone cyclically ever since.

Canned mackerel in tomato sauce is still popular in the United Kingdom and Scandinavia, and mackerel is a fairly common ingredient in sushi. Mackerel is full of healthy oils and is considered safer for regular consumption than some of the more popular fish, such as tuna and halibut.

When I was a kid, one of our neighbors would take his aluminum skiff out into the cove in front of our house as often as possible and bring home mackerel by the bucketful. Everyone for miles around had their freezers filled with cleaned and gutted mackerel. And though it is a tasty fish, there can be too much of a good thing. The local barn cats and herring gulls often had a feast when it came time to clean out the fridge at the end of the summer.

These mackerel fishermen are waiting to use their purse seine, seen with its cork floats forward of the helmsman.

SMOKED MACKEREL PÂTÉ

This flavorful spread is based on Ducktrap River Fish Farm's smoked mackerel. Ducktrap was founded in 1978 in Lincolnville, Maine, as a two-person trout-farming operation. After battling marauding raccoons, otters, skunks, and owls, which seemed to want the trout as much as they did, the owners built a four-by-four-foot smokehouse with an old woodstove and tried their hand at smoking seafood. They now have more than 145 employees and produce more than thirty-five smoked products, using all-natural ingredients, native hardwoods and fruit woods, and ecofriendly methods. This recipe is adapted from their cookbook, available from www.ducktrap.com. Serve this tasty Mediterranean spread on crisp toast or lightly toasted French bread.

1 pound brine-cured Greek, French, or Italian black olives, pitted

8 ounces Ducktrap River smoked mackerel

½ cup drained capers

1 small clove garlic, chopped

½ cup extra-virgin olive oil

2 tablespoons Metaxa or brandy

¼ bunch Italian parsley

Crusty bread or crackers, for serving

Lemon slices, for serving

1. Combine all the ingredients in a food processor and pulse very briefly, just until a coarse spread forms. (The tapenade can be prepared up to 1 week ahead. Pack it in a container, pour a thin layer of olive oil on top, and refrigerate. Bring to room temperature and stir before serving.)

2. Serve with crusty bread or crackers and lemon slices.

SERVES A CROWD!

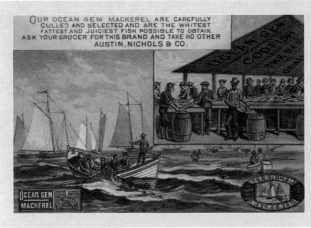

Ocean Gem mackerel: "the whitest, fattest and juiciest fish possible . . ."

GRILLED MACKEREL WITH CITRUS AND FENNEL

Mackerel is delicious when very fresh. It is very healthy with lots of omega-3 oils, is eco-friendly, and does not contain any contaminants.

½ teaspoon grated orange zest

½ teaspoon finely grated fresh
lemon zest

1½ tablespoons fresh lemon juice

Salt and pepper, to taste

⅓ cup extra-virgin olive oil

3 tablespoons finely chopped
fresh oregano, plus 4 large
sprigs

4 whole Atlantic mackerel, about
1 pound each

2 tablespoons vegetable oil

6 (¼-inch-thick) lemon slices

1 bulb fennel, sliced

Nonstick cooking spray

½ cup chopped flat-leaf parsley

1. Light a charcoal grill or preheat a gas grill.

2. Whisk the orange and lemon zests with the lemon juice, salt, pepper, and olive oil; whisk until combined well. Whisk in the chopped oregano. Measure out ½ cup of this mixture to brush on the fish while grilling.

3. Gut the fish and remove their heads. Score the mackerel vertically at 2-inch intervals on both sides, then brush them all over with the vegetable oil and season generously with salt and pepper. Season each cavity with salt and pepper, then place 2 lemon rounds, a quarter of the fennel slices, and an oregano sprig inside and close with skewers. If the lemon slices are too large to fit in the cavity, cut them in half horizontally.

4. Spray the grill rack with nonstick cooking spray and cook the mackerel for 5 to 7 minutes, depending on their size. Turn them over and continue grilling until they're just cooked through and flaky, about 3 to 5 minutes more. Remove them carefully from the grill using a spatula and tongs. Drizzle the remaining lemon-oil mixture over each fish, sprinkle with the parsley, and serve.

SERVES 4

> "To broil mackerel—clean and split them open; wipe dry; lay them on a clean gridiron, rubbed with suet, over a very clear slow fire; turn; season with pepper, salt and a little butter; fine minced parsley is also used."
>
> —*EARLY AMERICAN COOKERY: THE GOOD HOUSEKEEPER* BY SARAH JOSEPHA HALE (1841)

Salmon

When Pliny the Elder wrote nearly 2,000 years ago that "In Aquatania the Salmon surpasseth all the fishes of the sea," this wasn't news. Since prehistoric times, salmon have been appreciated, even revered. Salmon figure prominently in Native American legends, and their 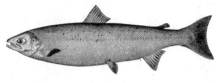 remains have been found at burial sites dating as far back as 25,000 years.

A life-size salmon carved on the overhang of Abri du Poisson in the Gorge d'Enfer in France may be as much as 35,000 years old. No one looking at that beautiful carving can doubt that the Cro-Magnon who carved it had a special relationship with this fish.

Unlike many other kinds of native fish, the early American settlers knew about salmon. It was highly valued in Britain and became much in demand in New England. In the eighteenth century salmon were caught in great numbers in the larger rivers in New England—the Connecticut and the Penobscot were two of the most abundant sources.

Unlike West Coast salmon, not all of the Atlantic fish die after spawning; some return to the sea. The young salmon stay in rivers and estuaries for about three years before leaving for salt water.

We think of depleted fisheries as a fairly recent phenomenon, but in fact the Atlantic salmon fishery was one of the very first to be wiped out by industrial activity in New England. Overfishing, the damming of rivers, and the release of effluents into waterways all took an early toll on such species as the salmon and shad that travel upriver to spawn. The salmon population of the Connecticut River was gone by the mid-1800s. Salmon survived in the Merrimac until later in the century and made their last stand on the Down East coast of Maine, where most of the catch was iced and shipped to Boston for sale.

By this time line fishing for salmon had long since given way to stationary nets. In Maine the small, open Lincolnville wherry was designed for inshore use to set the salmon nets and to retrieve the catch. The last New England fish house and equipment—which belonged to Robie Ames of Northport, Maine—are now on display at Mystic Seaport after seeing their last use in the 1940s, when the fish became so scarce that even a single family could not make a living from them. About this time canned Pacific Northwest salmon became popular, further reducing demand for Atlantic salmon.

According to an interview with Robie Ames preserved in Mystic Seaport's archives, he did not catch any salmon less than eight pounds; fish any smaller slipped through nets. Salmon ran up to sixteen or eighteen pounds, and averaged ten to twelve. The first salmon of the season were shipped to Faneuil Hall market in Boston.

"As food, fish is easier of digestion than meats are, with the exception of salmon; this kind of fish is extremely hearty food, and should be given sparingly to children, and used cautiously by those who have weak stomachs, or who take little exercise."

—*EARLY AMERICAN COOKERY: THE GOOD HOUSEKEEPER* BY SARAH JOSEPHA HALE (1841)

Thankfully, careful husbandry, research, and conservation efforts, as well as restocking using Atlantic salmon from Maine and Canada, have taken the fish off the endangered species list (although ironically, some stocks of the remaining salmon in Maine are considered endangered). Salmon are particularly amenable to aquaculture, and farmed fish are now readily available year-round. Norway and Chile are world leaders in farmed salmon, but Maine also has substantial salmon farms.

The wild salmon population is still struggling, but the Connecticut and Penobscot Rivers now have returning populations. In 2006 salmon could be caught on the Penobscot River on a catch-and-release basis.

There's good reason for salmon's ageless popularity. The flesh is firm and attractively pink-orange, while the flavor is pronounced but not fishy. They are particularly versatile: Salmon can be planked, grilled, baked, smoked, dried, or canned. They are high in vitamins A and B and omega-3 oils.

Mystic Seaport's Lincolnville wherry, a reproduction built in 1971.

SALMON WITH TRI-PEPPER SALSA

The *J. & E. Riggin*—part of the Maine windjammer fleet—is known for her excellent food. She was built in 1927 in Dorchester, New Jersey, as an oystering schooner and won the only oystering schooner race in 1929. Today owners Anne Mahle, an experienced boat cook, and her husband, Captain Jon Finger, serve their guests delicious dishes like this one, which appears in *At Home, At Sea: Recipes from the Maine Windjammer J. & E. Riggin.*

FOR THE TRI-PEPPER SALSA

½ red, green, and yellow bell
   pepper, seeded, julienned, and
   cut into 1-inch pieces

1 small red onion, cut in half and
   thinly sliced

3 tablespoons extra-virgin
   olive oil

Juice of 1½ limes

2 tablespoons chopped fresh dill

Salt and fresh-ground pepper,
   to taste

FOR THE SALMON

4–6 salmon fillets, 6 ounces each

¼ cup fresh lemon juice

¼ cup extra-virgin olive oil

¼ cup white wine

1 teaspoon salt

Fresh-ground black pepper,
   to taste

1. Make the Tri-Pepper Salsa: Toss the vegetables with the olive oil, lime juice, and dill.

2. Add salt and pepper to taste.

3. Allow the mixture to sit at room temperature for an hour (2 at the most—you don't want it to get soggy). Check the seasonings before serving.

4. Make the Salmon: Preheat the oven to 375°F.

5. Place the salmon fillets in a nonreactive 9x13-inch baking dish. Drizzle the fish with the lemon juice, olive oil, and white wine and season with salt and pepper. Let sit for 15 minutes to marinate.

6. Bake, uncovered, for 12 to 15 minutes. Remove the fish when it's still slightly darker in the center. It will continue to cook when you take it out of the oven.

7. Serve immediately topped with the Tri-Pepper Salsa.

SERVES 4-6

MISO-SOY GLAZED SALMON

Today we know salmon to be one of the healthiest foods around—full of omega-3 fatty acids, but low in calories and high in protein.

½ cup soy sauce

¼ cup miso paste

½ tablespoon toasted sesame oil

1 tablespoon brown sugar

2 tablespoons peanut oil

1 teaspoon chili-garlic sauce

1 shallot, minced

1 2-pound salmon fillet

1. Preheat the oven to 425°F.

2. Combine all ingredients except the salmon in a bowl. Refrigerate until ready to use.

3. Place the salmon on a baking sheet or glass baking dish and brush the fish generously with the glaze. Bake for 20 minutes or until it's opaque and just cooked through, and the glaze has browned and caramelized.

SERVES 6

Two prize-winning salmon recipes: salmon patties and salmon omelette.

BAKED SALMON WITH BLUE CRAB STUFFING
AND SWEET CHILI BUTTER

This terrific combination of flavors comes from the historic Captain Daniel Packer Inne in Mystic, Connecticut. I've sampled this in the restaurant, and it's delicious!

FOR THE CHILI BUTTER

1 chile pepper, diced with seed removed

1 tablespoon sugar

1 teaspoon garlic

1 teaspoon rice wine vinegar

8 tablespoons softened, salted butter

FOR THE SALMON AND STUFFING

½ cup celery stalks, diced

½ cup medium red onion, diced

½ cup mayonnaise

1 tablespoon Dijon mustard

1 egg, lightly beaten

1 teaspoon minced garlic

1 9-inch loaf French bread, cut into ½-inch cubes

4 salmon fillets, 8 ounces each, preferably thick cut

½ cup white wine

2 tablespoons lemon juice

1. Preheat the oven to 375°F.

2. Make the Chili Butter: In a small bowl, thoroughly combine all the chili butter ingredients.

3. Prepare the Salmon and Stuffing: In a bowl, combine the celery, onion, mayonnaise, mustard, egg, and garlic. Add the cubed bread and mix well.

4. Cut each salmon fillet into two layers lengthwise to create a pocket for the stuffing; be sure not to cut the top layer all the way through. Spoon the stuffing onto the bottom layer and fold the top half back over the stuffing.

5. Place the salmon in a baking dish, and pour wine and lemon juice atop. Bake for 15 to 20 minutes. Top with a dollop of the sweet chili butter and serve immediately.

SERVES 4

PEPPER-CRUSTED SALMON FILLETS IN
A CHANTERELLE-PLUM SAUCE

Lindbergh's Crossing is one of my very favorite restaurants. Located on Ceres Street in Portsmouth, New Hampshire, it's a bistro and wine bar housed in a brick-and-beam building that dates to the 1700s. Signatures on the beams attest to the building's long history as a ship's chandlery. The chef, Evan Mallett, created this wonderful dish to pair with some of his favorite wines: Pacific Pinot Noirs. As Evan says, this combination "sounds odder than it is." It doesn't seem odd to me—just delicious.

2 pounds salmon fillets

Pinch of salt

1 tablespoon mixed peppercorns, coarsely ground

3 plums

1 red onion

1 cup fresh chanterelle mushrooms

2 tablespoons olive oil

½ cup sherry

2 tablespoons brown sugar

1 teaspoon minced garlic

1. Preheat the oven to 450°F.

2. Season the salmon fillets lightly with salt and generously with mixed ground pepper. Refrigerate.

3. Halve the plums, remove the pits, and cut into even wedges. Peel, halve, and cut the onion into thin half-moon slices. Scrub the chanterelles with a dry brush to remove any dirt. Cut the larger ones in half.

4. In a heavy, nonreactive sauté pan, heat the olive oil until smoking. Carefully sear the seasoned side of the salmon fillets until golden brown. Remove to a baking sheet, seared-side up, and place in the preheated oven for 5 to 7 minutes.

5. Meanwhile reduce the heat to medium and add the mushrooms and onion. Stir the mushroom mix until the oil is absorbed.

6. Deglaze the pan with the sherry and stir for 2 minutes. Add the brown sugar, garlic, and plums and stir well until all the ingredients are incorporated and the plums are just soft.

7. Spoon the sauce over the salmon fillets and serve immediately.

SERVES 6

SMOKED AND CURED SALMON

Salmon is perhaps the most commonly smoked and cured fish in the world. Smoked salmon is a real delicacy and is now readily available in grocery stores and fish markets. It makes a wonderful and elegant hors d'oeuvre served on slices of cocktail rye with some mustard, finely chopped red onion, and a spring of dill.

There are two methods of smoking salmon—or any fish, for that matter: hot smoking and cold smoking. First, the fish are salted or brined and kept cool. Hot-smoked salmon is cooked at a higher temperature, generally between 120°F and 180°F. The temperature is gradually increased over a period of six to eight hours. In cold smoking, the fish is not actually cooked but cured in smoke with temperatures between 70°F and 90°F for a longer period. The texture of cold-smoked salmon is more like gravlax or lox. Hot-smoked salmon has a texture more like cooked fish.

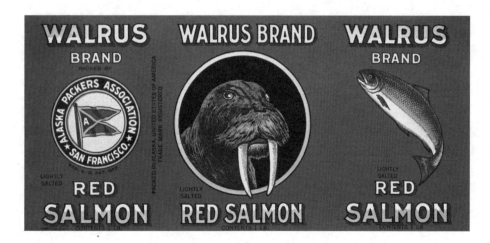

GRAVLAX

Gravlax is a traditional Scandinavian method of curing fish in a blend of salt, sugar, and dill. Although purists reject the idea, I have experimented with adding juniper berries, tarragon, aquavit, or even citrus vodka—with excellent results.

½ cup kosher salt

½ cup sugar

2 tablespoons cracked white
  peppercorns

2 teaspoons juniper berries

1-pound fresh salmon fillet,
  skin on

1 large bunch fresh dill, stems
  included

1. Mix the salt, sugar, white peppercorns, and juniper berries.

2. Take a handful of this mixture and rub it on both sides of the salmon. Place the salmon in a glass or other nonreactive dish, and sprinkle the rest of the mix on top.

3. Cover the salmon with dill, wrap it in plastic wrap, and return to the dish. Refrigerate for 48 hours, depending on how thick the salmon is and how salty you'd like it.

4. Slice the salmon off the skin and slice into thin slivers. Serve with your favorite mustard sauce.

SERVES 8 AS AN APPETIZER

SMOKED SALMON FRITTATA

A frittata is a sort of crustless quiche that combines all manner of meats, veggies, fish, or herbs and is finished under the broiler. It makes a lovely brunch or supper dish, or even an appetizer. There are endless varieties, but this one balances the smoky flavor of the salmon with herbs and vegetables.

2 tablespoons butter

1 leek, white part only, sliced
    thinly

1 cup sliced wild mushrooms,
    such as porcini or shiitake

1 shallot, chopped

8 eggs

⅓ cup light cream

4 ounces smoked salmon, flaked
    or cut into ½-inch pieces

2 tablespoons chopped fresh
    chives

2 tablespoons chopped fresh
    parsley

Salt and pepper

1 tablespoon olive oil

1. Heat the butter in a small sauté pan over medium heat. Add the leek, mushrooms, and shallot and sauté for 4 to 5 minutes, stirring occasionally. Set aside to cool.

2. Lightly beat the eggs with the cream in a large bowl. Stir in the smoked salmon, mushroom mixture, and herbs. Season with salt and pepper.

3. Heat the olive oil in a 10-inch nonstick skillet over medium heat; pour in the egg mixture. As the eggs start to cook, pull in the cooked edges with a spatula to allow the uncooked egg on top to move to the bottom of the pan for even cooking. When the frittata is almost set (firm but still somewhat liquid on top), place the pan under the broiler to finish cooking the top. Slide the frittata onto a cutting board and cut into wedges. Serve hot or at room temperature.

SERVES 6

Shad and Shad Roe

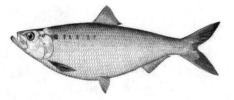

Massachusetts has its Sacred Cod, but the state of Connecticut has its shad. Although only designated as the state fish in 2003, shad was an important food source long before the first white settlers landed on New England shores. Native Americans saw shad as a seasonal gift and were known to have large springtime gatherings to roast these fish over open wood fires, often planking them (much the way salmon is prepared in the Pacific Northwest). The technique is used to this day in springtime Connecticut shad bakes.

Typically, among the early settlers, food that was in an overabundant supply and consumed by the Natives was viewed with skepticism. Like lobster and other bounties of the sea, in the early colonial days shad was considered poor people's food—fed to servants and used as fertilizer. Thousands of barrels of shad were shipped off to Revolutionary War troops and reputedly staved off hunger in some very lean times.

The fish themselves spend most of their lives in the ocean but begin to make their way up freshwater rivers in spring, when it comes time to spawn. Indeed, the return of the shad is such a reliable harbinger of springtime that the shad bush and the shad frog—both of which flourish in early spring—take their names from the species' return. Shad begin to appear in rivers of the Northeast as early as March; they show their faces in the Connecticut River between April and June. By summer the shad are headed back to sea.

Shad is a member of the herring family and is valued not only for its flavorful meat but also for its excellent roe. The biggest drawback to enjoying shad is the number of bones—some 1,300 in an adult fish, which grow to roughly thirty inches and typically weigh in at three to five pounds. And to make things even more challenging, the bones do not follow a neat pattern as they do in other bony fish, but run both horizontally and vertically. Old-time shad boners guarded their techniques carefully, and for most of us, buying boneless fillets—or getting invited to a Connecticut shad bake—is the best bet.

The Shad Shack in Haddam, Connecticut.

ROES BY ANY OTHER NAME . . .

Caviar is, of course, the queen of fish roe. It is the eggs of sturgeons, those prehistoric armored bottom feeders. The highest-quality caviar, like wildly expensive beluga, sevruga, and osetra, came historically from the Caspian or Black seas.

But in the past thirty years, the stock of sturgeon in the Caspian has plunged to 10 percent of its previous total, due to rampant overfishing. A United Nations ban on the export of most caviar (except Iranian) from the Caspian Sea has left true beluga caviar hard to find. Now other sources are taking up the slack, including American farm-raised caviar. Some experts predict that America will soon become a leading caviar producer once again.

Caviar is almost as famous for its astronomical prices as its exquisite, briny flavor. But this wasn't always the case. If you went in to a tavern in New York City in the early 1800s, you might well have been given a free supply of caviar so that its saltiness would encourage you to purchase more libations than you might have planned—much the way popcorn and salted nuts are served today in your neighborhood bar. In those days the Hudson and Delaware Rivers teemed with massive sturgeon, and caviar became known as "Albany beef." But by the early 1910s, the fishery was virtually nonexistent—the usual culprits of overfishing and environmental destruction had once again taken their toll.

The term caviar should really only apply to sturgeon roe, but you can find it applied to all kinds of roe—bowfin, whitefish, salmon, and paddlefish. Inexpensive jars of lumpfish and salmon roe, available in most grocery stores, make good caviar substitutes; mix them with sour cream or cream cheese and a squeeze of lemon to make a nice appetizer. Topping deviled eggs with caviar is also a great way to spruce up standard party fare.

Shad roe usually comes in two roughly symmetrical lobes surrounded by a thin membrane. Each lobe is generally considered enough for one serving. The roe is often wrapped in bacon, pan-fried or broiled, and served with lemon—or with scrambled eggs. Shad roe has a delicate flavor that bears little relation to the strong, briny taste of caviar.

Americans don't eat a lot of fish roes these days, but someone, somewhere eats just about every kind of roe: Herring, lumpfish, whitefish, flying fish, haddock, pollock, salmon, cod, lobster, tuna, urchin, and many more are all popular. The Japanese, Korean, and Scandinavian peoples may be the most enthusiastic roe consumers.

NEW POTATOES WITH CAVIAR AND CRÈME FRAÎCHE

You can buy crème fraîche in the supermarket, but making your own is simple. Combine 3 parts heavy cream and 2 parts yogurt or buttermilk in a glass bowl. Cover and let stand at room temperature for 12 hours, until thick and creamy.

12 small red new potatoes

¼ cup olive oil

Black pepper

½ cup crème fraîche

1 small jar lumpfish or caviar (be guided by your tastes and your budget!)

Fresh dill sprigs, for garnish

1. Preheat the oven to 350°F.
2. Rub the potatoes all over with the olive oil. Sprinkle with black pepper.
3. Bake the potatoes for 35 minutes or until just soft. Halve the potatoes and scoop out the insides, leaving the skins for a shell.
4. Mash the potato flesh with the crème fraîche, and spoon back into the shells. Top with caviar and a sprig of dill.

SERVES 12 AS AN HORS D'OEUVRE

"One can be unhappy before eating caviar, even after, but at least not during."

—ALEXANDER KORDA

CONNECTICUT BAKED STUFFED SHAD

This recipe is adapted from *The New England Yankee Cookbook*, published in 1939, and attributed to the "New England kitchen of Louise Crathern Russell."

1 large shad (about 5 pounds)

1 cup cracker crumbs

4 tablespoons melted butter

¼ teaspoon salt

¼ teaspoon pepper

1 small onion, minced

1 teaspoon sage

1 cup hot water

¼ pound sliced bacon

1. Preheat the oven to 400°F.

2. Make sure the fish has been cleaned and gutted, but leave its head and tail on. Rinse well and pat dry.

3. In a bowl, combine the cracker crumbs, butter, salt, pepper, onion, and sage. Stuff the cavity of the fish with this mixture and sew the edges together.

4. Place the fish on a rack in a baking pan. Add water to the pan. Lay the bacon slices over the shad.

5. Bake for 10 minutes at 400°F, then reduce the heat to 325°F and bake for another 30 minutes, basting frequently to keep the fish tender and well browned.

SERVES 6

BROILED SHAD ROE

This recipe is from *The Herald Tribune's Home Institute Cookbook,* a classic and best-selling American cookbook originally published in 1937.

3 pairs shad roe

8 tablespoons butter, melted

Salt and pepper, to taste

Lemon wedges

1. Preheat the oven to 400°F.

2. Brush the roe with the melted butter. Sprinkle with salt and pepper to taste, and broil for 5 minutes on each side.

3. Serve with Maître d'Hotel Butter (see the recipe below) and lemon wedges.

SERVES 6

MAÎTRE D'HOTEL BUTTER

Maître d'Hotel Butter is one of the most classic additions to fish of all kinds. It's simple and elegant, and brings out the best in fresh seafood. Store some in the refrigerator and use it on grilled or broiled fish.

8 tablespoons butter, room temperature

1 tablespoon minced parsley

1½ tablespoons lemon juice

½ teaspoon sea salt

Dash of white pepper

Cream the butter until soft. Add the remaining ingredients and beat until fluffy.

SAUTÉED SHAD ROE WITH APPLEWOOD BACON

Classic preparations for shad roe are generally pretty simple and often include bacon, which adds a nice salty, smoky touch.

2 strips apple-cured bacon

1 tablespoon butter

½ cup sliced shallots

¼ cup flour

½ teaspoon salt

Fresh-ground pepper

3 pairs shad roe

Chopped chives, for garnish

Lemon wedges, for garnish

1. Cook the bacon in a large frying pan until crisp. Remove the bacon and drain it on paper towels. Add the butter to the frying pan and melt.

2. Add the shallots and sauté until soft.

3. Mix the flour, salt, and pepper on a plate. Dredge the shad roe in this seasoned flour, shaking off any excess.

4. Increase the heat to medium and add the roe to the pan. Fry for about 5 minutes on each side, until golden brown.

5. Serve hot, with the pan juices poured over and garnished with crumbled bacon, chopped chives, and lemon wedges on the side.

SERVES 6

Smelts

In New England smelts have happy associations. Although they can be taken in winter from fish shacks on the ice, early spring is when the smelts run in the river mouths and are caught in great abundance with lines

and nets. So after the long winter when everybody's ready for a good party, a smelt fry is a coastal tradition. There are likely to be deep-fried smelts, sautéed smelts, baked smelts, smoked smelts—even pickled smelts.

Smelts are small fish, generally between six and nine inches long and slender, with a bright silver skin. They're most often eaten whole, the crispy tail being a particular favorite, although some people prefer to remove the backbone (which pulls out easily from the cooked fish). The other bones are so soft that other than adding a little texture, they are in no way unpleasant to eat.

The most common variety in the North Atlantic is the rainbow smelt. Although they have a high oil content, when fresh these fish have a light flavor and a scent that some say resembles cucumbers. Certain West Coast smelts are called candlefish: Their oil content is so high that Native Alaskans once dried them, inserted a twig for a wick, and burned them like candles!

Smelts are members of the herring family, as are the shad and alewives that they closely resemble. They were an important food source through the nineteenth century. Captain John Smith, that seventeenth-century explorer who promoted the wonders of New England back to his English homeland, claimed that fishermen here took twelve hogsheads (barrels) of alewives in one night. In the Massachusetts Fisheries Report of 1870, smelts were so plentiful in Boston's Back Bay that residents of "lower Beacon Street might be seen at early hours, eagerly catching their breakfast from their back door."

FRIED SMELTS

This is an Italian-influenced method of frying smelts.

1 cup Italian bread crumbs

½ cup freshly grated Pecorino
   Romano cheese

½ teaspoon sea salt

2 pounds smelts, dressed

2 eggs, lightly beaten

Vegetable oil for deep-frying

Lemon wedges, for serving

Tartar sauce, for serving

1. In a bowl, combine the bread crumbs, cheese, and salt.

2. Rinse the smelts and dry them thoroughly. Dip each piece into the beaten eggs and then dredge in the bread crumb mixture.

3. Dry the fish on a cake rack for 15 minutes so the breading can set.

4. Meanwhile, heat the oil to 365°F. When it's hot, deep-fry the smelts until golden brown, about 4 minutes. Drain on paper towels and serve with lemon wedges and tartar sauce.

SERVES 4-6

TO FRY SMELTS

"Smelts should be very fresh, and not washed more than is necessary to clean them. Dry them in a cloth, lightly flour, dip them in egg, and sprinkle over with very fine bread crumbs, and put them into boiling lard. Fry to a nice pale brown, and be careful not to take off the light roughness of the crumbs, or their beauty will be spoiled. Dry them before the fire on a drainer, and serve with plain melted butter. This fish is often used as a garnishing."

MRS. BEETON'S HOUSEHOLD MANAGEMENT (1861)

BOQUERONES
(PORTUGUESE-STYLE SMELTS)

Boquerones are a Spanish tapas, often made with anchovies marinated in vinegar. This delicious Portuguese-inspired dish is from Robert LaMoia, executive chef and owner of LaMoia Restaurant and Tapas Bar in Providence, Rhode Island. His menu is chock-full of authentic Portuguese seafood dishes and well worth a trip. Corn flour is also known as masa flour or masa harina, and can be found in the Hispanic foods section in most supermarkets.

½ cup corn flour

⅓ cup wheat flour

1 tablespoon salt

1 egg

¼ cup milk

¾ cup water

3 cups cornflakes

2 pounds smelts, dressed

Vegetable oil as needed for frying

2–3 tablespoons olive oil

1 tablespoon chopped garlic

½ teaspoon red pepper flakes

¼–½ cup sherry vinegar

1. Mix the corn and wheat flours with the salt. Beat in the egg and milk. Slowly add the water until the mixture resembles thin pancake batter.

2. Crush the cornflakes into small pieces, but don't pulverize them.

3. Wash and dry the smelts thoroughly. Dip them in the batter, then roll them in the cornflakes. You can proceed with cooking the smelts at this point, or refrigerate or even freeze them for later.

4. In a deep pot, heat the oil to 360°F. Drop the smelts into the hot oil a few at a time so as not to overcrowd them. Cook until golden brown. Remove the smelts from the oil and drain on paper towels.

5. Heat the olive oil in a frying pan. Add the garlic and red pepper and cook until sizzling—but don't let the garlic brown, as it will become bitter. Add the smelts to the pan and swirl to heat them.

6. Add the sherry vinegar and carefully ignite, allowing the flames to subside and the vinegar to evaporate. Serve the smelts immediately.

SERVES 4-6

Squid

In New England squid are mostly associated with Italian cuisine ("calamari"), but they are equally at home in Spanish and Portuguese dishes, including paella and squid in their ink. (As an aficionado of all things Portuguese, I would like to see squid become known by their Portuguese name *lula*—surely the prettiest of their names!)

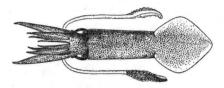

Squid are cephalopods, like octopuses and cuttlefish, which means that they aren't fin fish—or fish all at, really. They're actually shellfish, but not bivalves or crustaceans. So what are they doing in the "Fin Fish" section? Well, with apologies to any marine biologist who might be reading this, I like them so much I had to include them *somewhere*. And here they are.

Cuttlefish are much like squid but have a cuttlebone used for buoyancy—familiar to us from its use in canary cages. A memorable meal in Cuenca, Spain, was sautéed small cuttlefish stuffed with their own tentacles and accompanied by a sauce of their black ink. Cuttlefish, rather than squid, are often used in this preparation as they have more ink. (This ink, called sepia, used to be a valuable dye.) Most cuttlefish are imported into this country, and since their taste is so close to that of squid, they may not be worth their higher price.

Squid themselves come in sizes from one inch to sixty feet. It's only in the past few years, however, that live giant squid have been captured—two of them, both about twenty-five feet long. One of these examples is preserved in a tank at the National Museum of London. Larger dead squid have been found, and of course *much* larger ones exist in terrifying legends—including the Scandinavian "Kraken" tale of a giant squid attacking and sinking ships. Legend held that the Kraken was as much as a mile in circumference.

Most of the squid for the table are hardly giant, however. With a body length of two inches or so, they are cooked whole. Larger ones are usually cut into rings after removing the skin, head, and small mantle. Expecting the usual plateful of two-inchers, I was once taken aback to be served a single Portuguese *lula* of about nine inches long. It was tender and mild.

Squid is caught both for the table and as bait. It may be the most versatile bait in the ocean—species ranging from flounder to stripers to swordfish will all go for squid. It takes to freezing well, so it can be preserved for future use. Alas, what it doesn't tolerate is overcooking—it turns as chewy as a rubber band.

In New England most of the squid are caught by commercial draggers during April and May. Fishermen also jig for squid using specialized lures with two sets of multiple hooks. Squid are attracted to light, so some squidders shine bright lights into the water or fish near street lamps.

At the fish market, squid are sold already cleaned. If you're lucky enough to get some fresh ones, cleaning isn't difficult—but there is a knack to it. First remove the transparent quill under the mantle, then pull the head off; most of the guts will come with it. Pull off the skin, starting with one of the wings, and rinse. For more detailed instructions and tips, you can go to squidfish.net.

CALAMARI TRIZZANO

This is a recipe from Angela Sanfilippo, president of the Gloucester Fishermen's Wives Association, who came to Gloucester, Massachusetts, from Sicily in 1965. This association of determined women has played a vital role in protecting fishing grounds and went head-to-head with Big Oil when there was a proposal to drill for oil in Georges Bank. The women have also been a major force in developing balanced management plans for creating sustainable fisheries, as well as improving safety conditions aboard fishing vessels. Not exactly a coffee klatch! Nevertheless, the association's cookbook is a treasure.

⅓ cup olive oil

2 cups sliced onions

3 pounds cleaned calamari or squid, cut into rings

3 tablespoons pine nuts

3 tablespoons raisins

¼ cup fresh parsley

2 teaspoons salt

Black pepper, to taste

1 28-ounce can crushed tomatoes

Italian bread, for serving

1 pound spaghetti (optional)

Romano cheese (optional)

White rice (optional)

1. Heat the olive oil in a skillet and sauté the onions. Add the calamari and sauté until golden.

2. Add the nuts, raisins, parsley, salt, pepper, and crushed tomatoes. Cook over medium heat for about 20 minutes. Remove from the heat and let the mixture sit for 15 minutes.

3. Serve in individual bowls with Italian bread. If you'd like to serve with spaghetti, cook the pasta according to package directions. Drain and mix with the calamari sauce. Sprinkle with Romano cheese. This dish can also be served with white rice.

SERVES 5-6

CALAMARI FRITTI

Fried calamari is becoming more and more popular, especially in coastal seafood restaurants. It's often served with a tartar sauce or marinara sauce for dipping and is just great with a glass of cold beer or Italian white wine. I make mine with masa harina or golden corn flour.

Oil, for deep-frying

2 pounds small squid, cleaned

1 cup golden corn flour

1 teaspoon sea salt

½ teaspoon white pepper

2 teaspoons dried oregano

1 egg

Lemon wedges, for serving

Tartar or marinara sauce, for
   serving

1. In a deep pot, heat enough oil to easily accommodate the squid, bringing the temperature high enough so the calamari bubble briskly when you put them in.

2. Rinse and dry the squid thoroughly. Slice it into rings, leaving the tentacle portions whole.

3. Mix the dry ingredients on a plate or in a shallow bowl. In a separate bowl, beat the egg with a little water.

4. Dip the squid pieces into the egg mixture and then roll them in the flour mixture, shaking off any excess.

5. With a slotted spoon, carefully lower the squid into the hot oil. It will bubble quite a bit. Cook for 2 minutes or until just golden and cooked through. Drain on paper towels and serve with lemon wedges and your favorite sauce.

SERVES 6

MARINATED GRILLED SQUID SALAD

One summer I was the cook on a boat in Portugal. I had been to the municipal fish market that morning, and I was looking for a way to cook squid very quickly to serve as a cold supper on what was a very hot day. The following preparation is a little like the technique for escabeche: cooking quickly, then marinating. It's lovely with a simple green salad and bread.

2 pounds cleaned squid, whole

½ cup olive oil

¼ cup crushed garlic

1 tablespoon chopped fresh
   oregano

1 tablespoon grated lemon rind

2 shallots, finely sliced

¼ cup white wine

3 tablespoons red wine vinegar

Juice of 1 lemon

Sea salt and fresh ground pepper,
   to taste

1. Combine the squid, oil, garlic, and oregano. Let the squid marinate for up to an hour.

2. Preheat a gas or charcoal grill to high. Place the squid on the grill till they're cooked through and a tiny bit charred. Flip over and cook briefly on the other side.

3. In a bowl, combine the remaining ingredients. Slice the squid thinly into rings and add the cooked squid to the bowl. Toss and refrigerate until ready to serve.

SERVES 4–6

Swordfish

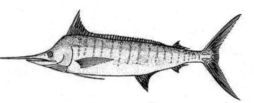

We are generally content not to know too much about where our food comes from. But two best-selling books, Sebastian Junger's *The Perfect Storm* and Linda Greenlaw's *The Hungry Ocean*, have thrust swordfishing, and commercial fishing in general, into the American consciousness. *The Perfect Storm* gave a riveting account of the dangers of fishing: small boats in unpredictable and occasionally violent weather, far from shore. *The Hungry Ocean* speaks eloquently to the question of why, in the twenty-first century, people still choose what has often been called "the world's most dangerous occupation."

(Of course, fishing has always been dangerous. Between 1870 and 1880 nearly 1,000 fishermen were lost at sea from Gloucester, Massachusetts, alone—a town with a population of only 15,000 souls.)

For some people, fishing is in their blood and their heritage. Some need the structure and the discipline of shipboard life: For them, life ashore is always teetering on the edge of disaster. Safety lies at sea. For others it's the elemental nature of fishing—the thrill of the chase—"killing fish" as Linda Greenlaw, considered by many to be the world's best swordboat captain, baldly put it. It's never the money. As Greenlaw's mentor explained to her, "If you're in it for the money, you're in the wrong business."

Greenlaw also has decided opinions on swordfish conservation. In *The Hungry Ocean* she writes that "U.S. fishermen are not pirates. . . . Fishermen of my generation are conservation minded. We are also frustrated that the public is being brainwashed with misinformation by a group of do-gooders. Fishing for a living is our heritage.

Consumers and seafood lovers should enjoy the fruits of the labor of law-abiding and conservation-minded fishermen without being made to feel guilty. Eat U.S.-caught swordfish! It's legal!"

Whatever your views about sustainability, it's generally agreed that fishing boats from other countries with less conservation-minded agendas have not helped the U.S. swordfishery much. This problem is exacerbated by the fact that swordfish are large and highly migratory. In the western Atlantic swordfish range from Canada as far south as Argentina. In the eastern Atlantic they range from Ireland to South Africa; they can also be found in the Indian and Pacific Oceans. The fact that these fish travel so widely and in so many international waters makes regulation that much more difficult. To further complicate matters, our demand for swordfish is so great that we end up importing a significant amount each year, and we can't be sure whether or not these fish have been caught in compliance with international regulations.

Government sources report that Atlantic swordfish are overfished but are not yet an endangered species. For all of us who love our swordfish, let's hope it never comes to that!

Swordfish are characterized by their long flat bill or sword. They have a prominent dorsal fin and reach a maximum size of fourteen feet long; they can weigh more than 1,000 pounds. The meat is firm and perfect for grilling. It stands up well to seasonings and sauces, but is wonderful just brushed with a little olive oil, seasoned with salt and pepper, and cooked briefly over hot coals.

THE *FLORENCE*

Mystic Seaport's dragger and summertime swordfishing boat *Florence* was built in 1926 just down the Mystic River below the drawbridge. At forty feet, *Florence* is only half the size of Linda Greenlaw's *Hannah Boden*—but then the fishery was different eighty years ago. Swordfish swimming on the surface were harpooned from the long pulpit that extended from *Florence's* bow. A line was attached to the harpoon and to a wooden keg, which went overboard when a fish was struck. Usually a dory was then launched to retrieve the fish. *Florence* did not have to go far offshore to find swordfish. Now swordfishing boats range far out into the Atlantic to set their lines of baited hooks. appropriately called longlines. The lines may run out as far as forty miles, with massive hooks spread at intervals along the line.

PAN-ROASTED SWORDFISH WITH MUSTARD-HERB CRUST

I recommend using a good nonstick pan for this dish to keep the crust from sticking.

1 tablespoon chopped Italian
  parsley

1 tablespoon chopped fresh
  oregano

1 tablespoon chopped fresh
  chives

2 teaspoons fresh thyme

1 tablespoon grated lemon zest

2 tablespoons horseradish
  mustard

2 tablespoons mayonnaise

2 tablespoons olive oil

1½ pounds swordfish steaks

Sea salt and pepper, to taste

1. In a bowl, whisk together the herbs, lemon zest, mustard, and mayonnaise.

2. Brush this mixture on the swordfish steaks and refrigerate for 20 minutes. Remove and let stand for 5 minutes.

3. In a nonstick skillet, heat the vegetable oil until it's hot but not smoking.

4. Add the swordfish steaks and cook until they're golden and crusty, about 4 to 5 minutes. Turn and cook for another 3 or 4 minutes, depending on thickness of the steaks. The fish should be just opaque throughout.

SERVES 4

GRILLED SWORDFISH WITH MINT GREMOLATA

Gremolata is a traditional garnish/flavoring added to osso bucco. It's a simple mixture of grated lemon rind, finely chopped or mashed garlic, and minced parsley. This wonderful combination is a natural for seafood, especially with the addition of aromatic mint leaves.

2 tablespoons finely chopped
   fresh flat-leaf parsley

1 tablespoon finely chopped fresh
   mint

2 teaspoons minced garlic (about
   2 large cloves)

1 tablespoon freshly grated
   lemon zest

5 tablespoons olive oil, divided

Sea salt, to taste

4 swordfish steaks, 6 ounces
   each

Freshly ground black pepper,
   to taste

1. Preheat a grill or broiler.

2. In a small bowl, stir together the gremolata ingredients (parsley through lemon zest) and 3 tablespoons of the olive oil, and season with salt.

3. Brush the swordfish steaks with the remaining olive oil and season with salt and pepper to taste. Grill over high heat for 4 to 5 minutes.

4. Flip the fish over and top the cooked side of each steak with gremolata. Cook for an additional 4 to 5 minutes, until the fish is opaque throughout. Serve immediately.

SERVES 4

"In 1931, the *Gloucester Times* published a photograph of the schooner *Mary D'Eon* with a swordfish impaled in its wooden bow. In 1967, the research submersible *Alvin* from Woods Hole Oceanographic Institution was hit by a swordfish off the east coast of Florida at a depth of 2,000 feet."

—MARGARET NAGLE, *UMAINE TODAY*

BLACKENED SWORDFISH

This classic Cajun dish was make famous by New Orleans chef Paul Prudhomme. You can buy really good Cajun blackening spices (including Chef Paul's own brand) in the grocery store, but you can also make your own. Just increase the quantities given here to make extra, which you can store in an airtight container. This recipe uses a heavy skillet, but grilling works well, too.

5 teaspoons paprika

1 teaspoon ground dried oregano

1 teaspoon ground dried thyme

1 teaspoon cayenne pepper (less or more to taste)

1 teaspoon garlic salt

½ teaspoon white pepper

½ teaspoon black pepper

4 swordfish steaks, 6 ounces each

1 cup butter, melted

1. Combine all the dry ingredients well. Dump onto a plate or shallow bowl.

2. Preheat a skillet—preferably cast iron—until very hot. This may take 5 minutes or so. You want the pan to be almost red hot.

3. Dip the steaks in melted butter and then coat both sides with the spice mixture. Place the steaks in the dry hot skillet (in batches, if necessary, so as not to crowd them) and cook for 2 minutes. Be careful—this will smoke a lot.

4. Flip the steaks over and cook the other side. Drizzle the remaining butter on the cooked side.

5. Cook for another 4 to 6 minutes, until they're just opaque throughout. Serve immediately, with any remaining butter poured over.

SERVES 4

Tuna

Until fairly recently, it was understandable to think that tuna (aka "tunafish") came only in those hockey-puck-shaped cans with names like StarKist and Chicken of the Sea. Certainly when I was a kid, tuna meant a can of tuna. It meant a tunafish sand- 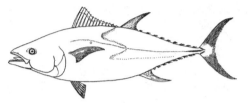 wich in my lunchbox. It never even occurred to me to that tuna might come fresh— and certainly not that it might be eaten raw. Health issues notwithstanding, I am now a devotee of fresh tuna: raw, barely seared, grilled rare—you name it. I know, I know. There are numerous health debates about tuna raw or cooked, but it hasn't killed me yet. It hasn't even made me sick. (Nor has my love of steak tartare, but that's a topic for another book.)

Actually canned tuna has an interesting history of its own. In 1903 Alfred P. Halfhill had a novel idea: He substituted canned tuna for canned sardines, the West Coast sardine stocks having suddenly disappeared. It was such a hit that it launched the San Diego offshore tuna-fishing fleet and later became a staple of soldiers in World War I. By the 1950s the United States was the leading producer of canned tuna.

In New England the tuna fishery relied not on canning but on fresh fish—both yellowfin and bluefin tuna. Sportfishing for tuna is an adventurous summertime activity—think *extreme fishing*. Commerically, many of the boats that fished for swordfish also fished for tuna. The rigging was the same, as was the technique—harpooning from a long pulpit off the bow of the boat. Mystic Seaport's fishing boat *Star*, built in 1950 in nearby Noank, is just such a vessel. For nearly thirty years she fished for both swordfish and tuna out of Montauk, New York.

In other parts of the world, tuna has been a favorite for thousands of years. Professor Daniel Levine noted in his speech "Tuna in the Ancient World" to the American

Institute of Wine and Food that "one of the earliest references to [tuna's] attractive flavor comes from the sixth-century B.C. Greek poet Hipponax, who wrote about a man who literally wasted his life by luxuriously overindulging in tuna with a savory sauce:

> For one of them, dining at his ease and lavishly every day on tuna and savory sauce [*myssotos*] like a eunuch from Lampsacus, ate up his inheritance; as a result he has to dig a rocky hillside, munching on cheap figs and coarse barley bread, fodder for slaves.

Tunny fish, as it was known in the 1800s, was prized as a rare catch, especially by Mediterranean immigrants. The relatively few people who had access to fresh tuna seemed to value it, but it wasn't until canning became an option and the Pacific tuna fishery and canneries began to thrive in the 1920s that it become a common addition to the American diet. Just image the 1950s and '60s without tuna casseroles!

While tuna does make an excellent sandwich or casserole (tuna casserole is kind of a retro guilty pleasure of mine), tuna is once again haute cuisine. Sushi, sashimi, grilled, baked, marinated—tuna is once again the delicacy that the ancient Greeks appreciated.

Delicious and convenient. Canned fish!

TUNA TARTARE IN ENDIVE BOATS

If you are a sushi fan, you'll love this simple hors d'oeuvre. Use only the best sushi-grade tuna.

½ pound sushi-grade tuna

¾ teaspoon grated fresh ginger

3 tablespoons tamari

1 teaspoon wasabi paste (or more
   to taste)

1 tablespoon rice wine vinegar or
   sushi vinegar

4 scallions, chopped

18 Belgian endive leaves, sepa-
   rated and washed

1. Chop the tuna into small pieces—about a ¼-inch dice. Gently mix in the remaining ingredients, except endive leaves.

2. Place a spoonful of the tartare on each endive leaf. Serve chilled.

MAKES 18 HORS D'OEUVRES

SAM HAYWARD'S TUNA AND GREEN BEAN SALAD

Sam Hayward is the executive chef at the award-winning Portland, Maine, restaurant Fore Street. This is his unique take on a classic *salade Niçoise*. The tuna is "marinated" overnight and then baked in extra-virgin olive oil and served with lightly cooked green beans and fresh summer lettuce. Plan on making the tuna a day or two ahead of time.

FOR THE TUNA

1 pound very fresh tuna,
    preferably yellowfin

1½ tablespoons Maine sea salt

Freshly ground black pepper

2 cloves garlic, very thinly sliced

A few fresh thyme sprigs

About 1–2 cups extra-virgin
    olive oil

FOR THE BEANS AND VINAIGRETTE

8 ounces green beans, ends
    trimmed

3 tablespoons sherry vinegar

¾ cup extra-virgin olive oil

Salt and fresh black pepper,
    to taste

2 tablespoons chopped summer
    garden herbs, such as flat
    parsley, thyme, rosemary,
    marjoram or oregano, mint, etc.

3 cups fresh summer lettuce,
    such as bibb, reine des glaces,
    lolla rosa, salad bowl, etc.

1. To Prepare the Tuna: Place it in a bowl or plastic container and rub with the salt and pepper. Toss the garlic and thyme sprigs on top, cover tightly, and refrigerate for 24 to 48 hours, turning the fish at least once.

2. Preheat the oven to 300°F. Place the tuna in a baking dish or shallow roasting pan and cover with the olive oil. Bake for 15 minutes. Reduce the oven temperature to 275°F and bake for about 45 minutes. The tuna is done when it flakes easily when tested with a fork. Cool the tuna in the fat; refrigerate after it comes to room temperature.

3. To Prepare the Beans: Fill a pot with lightly salted water and bring it to a boil over high heat. Cook the beans for 2 minutes; drain and place in a bowl of ice-cold water. Drain again.

4. To Prepare the Vinaigrette: Whisk together the vinegar, oil, salt, pepper, and herbs in a bowl.

5. Remove the tuna from the oil and break it into large pieces.

6. Toss the beans with the lettuce, adding enough of the vinaigrette to lightly coat the leaves. Arrange on a serving plate. Add the tuna on top and drizzle with a little of the vinaigrette. Serve any additional vinaigrette on the side.

SERVES 4-6

SEARED TUNA IN A BLACK AND WHITE SESAME CRUST

I like my tuna quite rare (or even raw), but if you prefer your fish cooked through, just turn the heat down and continue cooking until the inside is opaque.

6 tablespoons soy sauce, divided

2 tablespoons toasted sesame oil

1 teaspoon ginger paste (available in the Oriental food sections of many markets)

1 pound sushi-grade tuna steak, 1–1½ inches thick

3 tablespoons black sesame seeds

3 tablespoons white sesame seeds

1 teaspoon peanut oil

Wasabi, to taste

1. In a bowl, whisk together 2 tablespoons of the soy sauce, along with the sesame oil and ginger paste.

2. Cut the tuna into rectangular "logs" 1 to 1½ inches wide, 1½ inches high, and about 4 inches long. Thoroughly coat the tuna in the soy mixture. Cover and refrigerate for up to an hour.

3. In a wide bowl or on a plate, combine the black and white sesame seeds.

4. Rub a cast-iron or other heavy skillet with the peanut oil and heat until very hot.

5. Using tongs, add the tuna to pan and cook for just 2 minutes on each side, until the outside is crisp and the inside is rare. Serve with the remaining soy sauce and wasabi as you would for sushi.

SERVES 4

Treasures from the Deep

A few years ago I toured the Portland, Maine, fish co-op—a sort of clearinghouse for the commercial boats that fish out of that area. The catch from each boat is unloaded, sorted into big plastic tubs by vessel and species, and examined by a group of wholesale buyers; then an auction is held. I spotted hundred-pound halibut, cod, and haddock, but also other fish I didn't recognize. When I asked my guide about some of these species, he said, "Oh, those are redfish. They're considered trash fish." And the price paid at auction for these species was considerably lower than for the better-known fish, proving once again that one man's trash is another man's treasure.

Consumer demand is indeed higher for what people recognize. But there are a number of chefs out there who are working hard to introduce lesser-known types of fish to their customers. This is a great thing, in my view—not only do we get to eat more adventurously and with greater variety, but the more different types of fish we eat, the more likely we are to be able to balance consumer demand with sustainable fisheries.

There are some wonderful varieties of fish out there. You may not be able to find them as easily as the more popular species, but you can ask your fishmongers to pick some up for you if they run across any. The staff at one of my favorite local fish markets, York Lobster and Seafood in York, Maine, make a trip to the Boston wholesale fish pier every other day, and they're happy to accommodate special orders. You can also take a trip there yourself—cash on the barrelhead only, however, for retail customers.

Some of the species that I hope to see grow in popularity are wolffish (like monkfish, not a beauty, but excellent eating), tilefish, shark, skate, and redfish, or ocean

Randall Gandy, the all-important cook on the *L. A. Dunton* when she arrived at Mystic Seaport in 1963.

perch. Somehow, people in other parts of the world have accepted and enjoyed a greater variety of seafood than Americans have. I hope this will change. If you'd like to know more about the incredible range of seafood in the North Atlantic, I highly recommend Alan Davidson's encyclopedic book *North Atlantic Seafood*. It is an eye-opener and will give you a whole new appreciation of the bounty of our oceans.

MONKFISH

Monkfish's growing popularity and appearance on top restaurant tables has put this once abhorred fish into vogue. But it's still a long shot for the average grocery store customer. I was delighted to find monkfish at my local supermarket here in Maine—only to find that it was off the shelves a week later since it just wasn't selling. "I guess it's too weird," said the young man at the fish counter. It would no doubt be a very tough sell in other part of the country if it doesn't do well here, an area full of seafood aficionados.

The poor monkfish won't be winning any beauty contests, but fortunately looks aren't everything. The boneless tail meat has become highly prized by American chefs, though it has been given its due in Europe for many years. What used to be known as poor man's lobster is no longer poor man's anything, with top chefs getting top dollar for their monkfish creations. It just isn't getting snapped up by too many home cooks—yet.

Until recently, fishermen who landed monkfish generally threw them back—they were just too ugly to keep, much less eat. And face-to-face with one, you can certainly understand the impulse. Also known as goosefish, monkfish are mostly head and mouth—they possess a huge gaping maw that can eat up just about anything that comes its way, from other fish to crustaceans and even seabirds. The percentage of edible meat to total body weight is small, another disincentive for fishermen.

The lower part of the monkfish's jaw protrudes like a bad underbite. Both upper and lower jaws have long, needlelike teeth that point inward and can cause a nasty bite for anyone trying to land one of these fish without caution. Rising off the forehead of the fish is its very own fishing rod, a spine with a fleshy lobe at the end that the fish can arc forward and dangle in front of its jaws to lure in prey—hence one of monkfish's other names, anglerfish. They are voracious and insatiable feeders and have been known to consume everything from whole salmon to otters and cormorants. They are a mottled brown on top with a light underbody. They can grow to a length of about four feet and weigh up to fifty or sixty pounds.

Apart from their disproportionately large heads, monkfish are fairly flat, bottom-dwelling creatures whose culinary value is in the tail meat. Boneless except for the spine, they're easy to clean. The fillets from either side of the hind end of the fish are the choice portions. Browne Trading Company, located on Merrill's Wharf in Portland, Maine, may be the leading purveyor of seafood to the nation's top restaurants. The company's products appear on the very finest tables in the country. On a tour of the facility, I was treated to the sight of a whole monkfish ready for cleaning—not a pretty picture. But the tails I took home that evening were just gorgeous, grilled to perfection and seasoned with tandoori spices.

With its firm but tender texture and unmatched flavor, this is a versatile fish that can be grilled, baked, stewed, or poached. Monkfish liver is also considered a delicacy and is often served sashimi style in Japan. The tails sometimes come with a transparent membrane around them, easily removed with a small, sharp knife.

TANDOORI GRILLED MONKFISH

Monkfish's firm and flavorful flesh stands up well to the spice blend in this Indian-inspired dish.

2 cloves garlic, minced

1½ teaspoons grated ginger

1 teaspoon grated lime zest

1½ teaspoons ground cumin

1 teaspoon ground coriander

½ teaspoon ground turmeric

1½ pounds monkfish fillets or "tails"

2 tablespoons peanut oil

Salt and pepper, to taste

¾ cup plain yogurt mixed with 2 tablespoons chopped fresh cilantro

1. Light a charcoal grill or preheat a gas grill.

2. In a glass baking dish, combine the garlic, ginger, lime zest, and spices.

3. Brush the fish with the peanut oil and rub the spice mixture evenly over the fillets. Season to taste. Refrigerate for 15 minutes.

4. When the grill is hot, grill the monkfish for 5 to 7 minutes on each side, or until it's firm and opaque throughout. Slice into pieces and serve with a dollop of herbed yogurt on the side.

SERVES 4-6

BOUILLABAISSE

This recipe really could go just about anywhere in this book. Bouillabaisse is such an inclusive concoction that you can use a wide variety of ingredients. Traditionally, it contains fish and shellfish. The great debate is whether or not you can make "authentic" bouillabaisse without racasse, a Mediterranean fish not easily found outside that region. But in my view, bouillabaisse originated with the catch of the day— or perhaps even the by-catch or what didn't sell that day. Recipes I've read have included lobster, crab, squid, shrimp, eel, and octopus. Think of this recipe as an outline; include your favorites and use your imagination! This is traditionally served with rouille—garlicky red pepper mayonnaise—over slices of baguette in the bottom of the bowl. I like the bread on the side to sop up the juices.

¾ cup extra-virgin olive oil

1½ cups leeks, sliced into
    ¼-inch rounds

1 cup chopped onion

6 cloves garlic, mashed and
    chopped

1 tablespoon chopped Italian
    parsley

1 tablespoon fresh thyme leaves

1 bay leaf

1 teaspoon grated orange rind

1 28-ounce can Italian plum
    tomatoes

1½ quarts (6 cups) fish or
    seafood stock

½ cup white wine

Pinch of saffron, or to taste

1 pound monkfish (or any other
    firm white fish)

1 pound cod, cusk, hake, or
    other from the cod family

12 cherrystone or littleneck clams,
    cleaned

18 mussels, debearded and rinsed

1. Heat the olive oil in a stockpot. Sauté the leeks, onion, garlic, herbs, and orange rind until just fragrant.

2. Add the tomatoes with their juices and the fish stock. Add wine and saffron and stir. Bring to a boil, turn down, and simmer for 8 to 10 minutes.

3. Add the firm fish, like monkfish, first, and cook for 2 to 3 minutes. Then add the cod or other more delicate fish and bring to a simmer.

4. Add the clams and cook for 2 minutes. Add the mussels and cook till they open, about 5 more minutes.

5. Serve in large bowls, dividing the broth and seafood equally.

SERVES 6

SKATE

Skate and stingrays are related species in the same family as sharks. They're characterized by their flat bodies with "wings" on either side and a longish tail. Stingrays are named for the stinging barbs at the ends of their tails. It's said that some unscrupulous sellers used to stamp "scallops" out of skate wings—a practice unlikely to continue these days, given regulations. Skate is considered a wonderful and important part of the menu in France, where it's known as *raie*. It can be difficult to find here but is well worth the search; its delicate flavor is reminiscent of haddock and flounder.

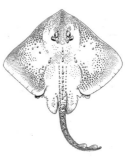

SAUTÉED SKATE WINGS WITH WHITE WINE AND CAPERS

Chef Jason Kennedy of Browne Trading Company in Portland, Maine, shared this wonderful skate recipe with us. He recommends serving it with sautéed asparagus on the side. It's fast, simple, and delicious.

3 tablespoons olive oil

¾ pound of skate wings or fillets, skin off (your fishmonger should be able to do this for you)

⅓ cup flour, seasoned with salt and fresh black pepper

Juice of 1 lemon

½ cup dry white wine

1 tablespoon capers, rinsed

2 tablespoons butter

Salt and pepper, to taste

1. Add the olive oil to a sauté pan over medium heat and preheat oven to 400°F.

2. While the pan is getting hot, dredge the skate fillets in seasoned flour. When the pan starts to smoke, gently place the floured skate fillets in the pan.

3. The skate should cook 2 to 3 minutes per side until golden brown. When turning the skate, be very gentle so as not to break the fillet. Finish the skate in the oven for about 5 minutes at 400°F.

4. Degrease the pan and place it back on the stove over medium heat. Add the lemon juice, white wine, and capers. Reduce this until almost dry, then add the butter, stir until melted, and season with salt and pepper. Remove the skate from the oven and pour the pan juices over. Serve immediately.

SERVES 2

WOLFFISH

It would be hard to say whether wolffish or monkfish would take home the Ugliest Fish Prize. At least the wolffish has a shape more commonly associated with a fish, though it still has a face only a mother could love. Its large mouth is equipped with huge canines  and massive molars. Still, this equipment is what allows for the wolffish's diet of clams, mussels, whelks, crab, and lobster, and hence its incredible lobsterlike taste and firm white flesh, sometimes marketed as ocean catfish. I urge you to give this underrated fish a try.

CRISPY COCONUT WOLFFISH

This recipe comes originally from *The Gloucester Fishermen's Wives Cookbook,* from the kitchen of Gerolama Parco Lovasco.

1 cup all-purpose flour

½ cup toasted coconut

1 egg

1 tablespoon milk

1 pound wolffish, cut into bite-size pieces

Oil, for frying

Chinese duck sauce, for serving

1. Mix together the flour and coconut.

2. In a separate bowl, combine the egg and milk. Beat well.

3. Dip the fish pieces into the egg mixture, then into the flour mixture, covering all sides of each piece.

4. Heat the oil in a skillet until it's quite hot. Fry the fish until golden brown. Serve with duck sauce.

SERVES 4

Photo Credits

Page 138 Mystic Seaport

Page 141 Mystic Seaport

Page 142 Mystic Seaport, 1983-3-11

Page 143 NorthEast Fisheries Science Center

Page 144 Mystic Seaport

Page 149 Mystic Seaport, 94-3-12

Page 150 NorthEast Fisheries Science Center

Page 151 Mystic Seaport, 75.291

Page 152 Mystic Seaport

Page 154 NorthEast Fisheries Science Center

Page 156 Mystic Seaport, 1994.381

Page 158 Mystic Seaport

Page 161 Mystic Seaport

Page 164 NorthEast Fisheries Science Center

Page 165 Nancy Freeborn

Page 167 Shutterstock © Dmitry Grishin

Page 172 NorthEast Fisheries Science Center

Page 175 NorthEast Fisheries Science Center

Page 180 NorthEast Fisheries Science Center

Page 182 Spencer Smith

Page 186 NorthEast Fisheries Science Center

Page 187 Mystic Seaport

Page 188 NorthEast Fisheries Science Center

Page 192 Mystic Seaport, 87-7-11

Page 193 NorthEast Fisheries Science Center

Page 197 NorthEast Fisheries Science Center

Page 198 NorthEast Fisheries Science Center

Resources

Mrs. Beeton's Household Management, 1861

Craig Claiborne, *Craig Claiborne's The New York Times Food Encyclopedia*, 1985

Lydia Marie Child, *The American Frugal Housewife*

Compleat American Housewife, Being a Collection of the Most Approved Recipes of the American Colonies, 1787

Alan Davidson, *North Atlantic Seafood: A Comprehensive Guide with Recipes*, 2003

Chris Dubbs, *The Quick and Easy Art of Smoking Food*, 1991

Fannie Merritt Farmer, *The 1896 Boston Cooking School Cook Book*

M. F. K. Fisher, *The Art of Eating*, 1990

Roger Fitzgerald, *Off the Hook: Reflections and Recipes from an Old Salt*, 2002

Mrs. Glasse, *The Art of Cookery Made Plain and Easy*, 1776

George Brown Goode, *The Fisheries and Fishery Industries of the United States*, 1884

Gloucester Fishermen's Wives Association Cookbook

Linda Greenlaw, *The Hungry Ocean: A Swordboat Captain's Journey*, 1999

Linda and Martha Greenlaw, *Recipes from a Very Small Island*, 2005

Sarah Josepha Hale, *Early American Cookery: The Good Housekeeper,* 1841

A Hard Racket for Living (film and audio), 1948

Sebastian Junger, *The Perfect Storm*, 1997

John M. Kochhiss, *Oystering from New York to Boston*, 1974

Mark Kurlansky, *The Big Oyster: History on the Half Shell*, 2006

Mark Kurlansky, *Cod*, 1997

A. J. McClane, *The Encyclopedia of Fish and Cookery*, 1977

Anne Mahle, *At Home, At Sea: Recipes from the Maine Windjammer J. & E. Riggin*, 2004

Maine Fishermen's Wives Association, *Seafood Cookbook Volume 1*, 1986

Maine Lobster Promotion Council

Carleton Mitchell, *The Winds Call: Cruises Near and Far*, 1971

New York Herald Tribune, Home Institute Cookbook, 1947

Mystic Seaport

NorthEast Fisheries Science Center

Sandra L. Oliver, *Saltwater Foodways: New Englanders and Their Food, at Sea and Shore, in the Nineteenth Century*, 1995

Susan Pollack, *The Gloucester Fishermen's Wives Cookbook: Recipes and Stories*, 2005

Amelia Simmons, *The First American Cookbook: A Facsimile of "American Cookery,"* 1796, 1958

Evalene Spencer, *Encyclopedia of Fish Cookery*, 1934

Keith Stavely and Kathleen Fitzgerald, *America's Founding Food: The Story of New England Cooking*, 2004

Lily Haxworth Wallace, *The Rumford Complete Cook Book*, 1928

Imogene Wolcott, *The New England Yankee Cookbook*, 1939

Colin Woodward, *The Lobster Coast: Rebels, Rusticators, and the Struggle for a Forgotten Frontier*, 2004

WEB SITES

www.blue-crab.org
www.fishingworks.org
www.squidfish.net

METRIC CONVERSION TABLES

APPROXIMATE U.S.–METRIC EQUIVALENTS

LIQUID INGREDIENTS

U.S. MEASURES	METRIC	U.S. MEASURES	METRIC
¼ tsp.	1.23 ml	2 Tbsp.	29.57 ml
½ tsp.	2.36 ml	3 Tbsp.	44.36 ml
¾ tsp.	3.70 ml	¼ cup	59.15 ml
1 tsp.	4.93 ml	½ cup	118.30 ml
1¼ tsp.	6.16 ml	1 cup	236.59 ml
1½ tsp.	7.39 ml	2 cups or 1 pt.	473.18 ml
1¾ tsp.	8.63 ml	3 cups	709.77 ml
2 tsp.	9.86 ml	4 cups or 1 qt.	946.36 ml
1 Tbsp.	14.79 ml	4 qts. or 1 gal.	3.79 lt

DRY INGREDIENTS

U.S. MEASURES		METRIC	U.S. MEASURES	METRIC
17 ⅗ OZ.	1 LIVRE	500 G	2 OZ.	60 (56.6) G
16 OZ.	1 LB.	454 G	1¾ OZ.	50 G
8⅞ OZ.		250 G	1 OZ.	30 (28.3) G
5¼ OZ.		150 G	⅞ OZ.	25 G
4½ OZ.		125 G	¾ OZ.	21 (21.3) G
4 OZ.		115 (113.2) G	½ OZ.	15 (14.2) G
3½ OZ.		100 G	¼ OZ.	7 (7.1) G
3 OZ.		85 (84.9) G	⅛ OZ.	3½ (3.5) G
2⅘ OZ.		80 G	1/16 OZ.	2 (1.8) G

Index

About the Authors

Jean Kerr's first food column appeared in the 1980s in *re:Ports Arts* and *Entertainment Weekly*. She was previously the food editor for *Portsmouth Magazine* and a regular contributor to *ACCENT* magazine. She is currently the editor of *Taste Magazine*, a food and wine magazine covering northern New England. She is also the author of the forthcoming *Union Oyster House Cookbook* and *Windjammer Cooking*.

Spencer Smith is a publishing executive based in Maine. He was the Editor of *Fodor's Seaside America* and *The Yachtsman's Winterbook*. He served as a board member of the National Maritime Historical Society and has worked on book publishing projects at South Street Seaport Museum and Mystic Seaport.